LEARNING ENVIRONMENT

INSPIRATIONAL ACTIONS, APPROACHES, AND STORIES FROM THE SCIENCE CLASSROOM

JARED FOX

Beacon Press
Boston

Beacon Press
Boston, Massachusetts
www.beacon.org

Beacon Press books
are published under the auspices of
the Unitarian Universalist Association of Congregations.

28 27 26 25   8 7 6 5 4 3 2 1

This book is printed on acid-free paper that meets the uncoated paper ANSI/
NISO specifications for permanence as revised in 1992.

Text design by BookMatters

*Library of Congress Cataloguing-in-Publication Data
is available for this title.*
Hardcover ISBN: 978-0-8070-2024-1
E-book ISBN: 978-0-8070-2025-8
Audiobook: 978-0-8070-2223-8

The authorized representative in the EU for product safety and compliance is
Easy Access System Europe 16879218, Mustamäe tee 50, 10621 Tallinn, Estonia:
http://beacon.org/eu-contact

For the WHEELS family

Contents

Foreword

In the world of education, the greatest reward does not come from accolades or achievements but from witnessing students step into their brilliance. The most profound of these moments are usually years after the student has left your classroom. It is then that you get the most honest assessment of your impact. They tell you directly about how it felt to be a student in your classroom and reveal the essence of your pedagogy. If the student remembers your jokes or the way you made them feel, you realize that your pedagogy is revealed through your sense of humor or the emotional context you provide in the classroom. If they remember your field trips or excursions, your pedagogy is revealed in the journeys you took them on. These experiences offer us the most beautiful insight into what is important to our work as teachers, even though they don't come as often as we would like.

For me, the work of Jared Fox, an educator, advocate, and innovator who was once my doctoral student, reveals what is most important about teaching. Jared has taken me on an educational journey that mirrors the ethos and urgency of reimagining education, something I have always believed in. He is, in many ways, a former student highlighting the essence of what I believe about teaching and learning, even as he makes his own mark on the framework of education. He has, in many ways, taken it up a notch, giving something powerful back to me and the field of science education and education writ large.

What Jared presents here is not merely a series of lessons or teaching anecdotes; it's an offering. This book unveils a framework that integrates student identity and voice into every aspect of learning, with New York City serving as a backdrop to transformation. Teaching in New York is not like teaching in any other place—the city's a living, breathing entity that challenges and inspires. Through its challenges and opportunities, it offers an exemplar for teaching anywhere. In this book, Jared has embraced a dynamic landscape to create opportunities where his students are not passive recipients of knowledge but active participants in crafting their understanding of the world. This is the very essence of a "STEM, STEAM, Make Dream" approach—where the boundaries of traditional education dissolve, making way for students to see themselves as scientists, engineers, activists, and creators in a space that reflects their realities.

Education, at its heart, is about cultivating connections—bridging differences to create spaces where every student feels valued, seen, and empowered. As you'll see in the pages ahead, Jared doesn't just teach science; he invites students into a community where they are co-creators of their learning experiences. His approach combines a deep commitment to environmental justice with practices that allow students to shape the classroom into a space that respects their unique perspectives and backgrounds. He is offering us a way to explore connection-making—between the animate and inanimate; and with students, with colleagues, with the environment, and with ourselves.

Jared's practice incorporates teaching methods I've long advocated, including drawing on the power of dialogue and having structured, reflective conversations with students that are more than just feedback sessions—they are transformative acts. By inviting his students to share their insights openly, Jared connects with them across cultural, social, and economic boundaries. Rather than waiting for an uncertain reward from students that left the classroom long ago, Jared's teaching opens the possibility for how these outcomes can be accomplished in the now. His approaches build trust and invite students to take part in shaping their own educational journeys while enhancing their teacher's practice. The power of this work is most consistently evident in the instructional models that dissolve the traditional hierarchies in the classroom, fostering mutual respect and shared responsibility.

If one were to ask me what the greatest gift of this book is, I would say it's the beautiful way it deepens the teacher's understandings of students and their experiences while offering tangible insights to improve teaching practices, foster stronger relationships, enhance classroom culture, and uplift the overall school environment and teaching profession. I loved reading about the ways that Jared and his students co-developed strategies to support both social-emotional and academic needs, creating a classroom atmosphere that's responsive to the students' lived realities. As I explore in my book *Ratchetdemic*, classrooms that embrace these approaches to teaching become spaces of authenticity where students can bring their full identities. Jared's classroom reflects this philosophy, blending rigorous academic work with a deep commitment to understanding his students beyond the walls of the school.

For Jared, teaching is as much about community as it is about content. His students aren't learning in a vacuum; they're examining issues like water conservation and plastic waste in the context of their own lives. With the city as both backdrop and subject, Jared creates lessons that are grounded in the real world. From field trips to the Bronx River to expert-led dialogues, he uses the city's challenges as a springboard for scientific inquiry, helping students see that the knowledge they gain can have a real impact on their communities. In these pages, you'll find descriptions of classroom activities and projects that invite students to see themselves as part of the solution—as empowered individuals who are capable of tackling environmental and social challenges.

Throughout our time together, Jared has always sought to push the boundaries of traditional education, making room for students who might otherwise feel marginalized or disengaged. His work aligns deeply with my ethos of making science and technology accessible, relatable, and meaningful. In his work, science isn't an abstract subject reserved for someone else; it's a tool to be used to understand and shape the world. Through the examination of local and global issues, the classroom becomes a place where students not only learn content but also develop a sense of agency and purpose. I am often asked to recommend a good book on how to simultaneously engage a classroom with overachievers, multilingual learners, quiet thinkers, and outspoken leaders. How do you co-create a vision for the classroom with students? How do you set goals and norms that reflect collective aspirations? How do you teach science in a way that connects to the real world? Now, I have a text I can point to.

In *For White Folks Who Teach in the Hood . . . and the Rest of Y'all Too*, I emphasize the need for teachers to engage with students in ways that respect their identities, experiences, and voices. Jared's inspiring approach makes meaning of this priority and brings it to the everyday practice of the educator. As you take in this masterful work, know that you're exploring a model for education that goes beyond standards, assessments, and curriculum. This book is a testament to what's possible when we view education as a collaborative, evolving process, and through reading it, we learn how to support students in thinking critically, working collaboratively, and approaching the world with a sense of purpose. This must-read is an invitation for all of us—educators, policymakers, and community members—to reimagine what schools can be. It is a reminder that our classrooms, like the cities that surround them and the students that learn within them, are brimming with potential. With the actions, approaches, and stories from *Learning Environment* guiding us, it is now up to us to fulfill it.

Christopher Emdin

Introduction

It's Time to Go to School

Firmly gripping the handlebars of my bicycle, I step over its frame and settle into its saddle. Quickly scanning my surroundings, I see a gap in the oncoming traffic and push one foot off the curb. In a quick and powerful motion, I crank my feet down onto the pedals, turning potential energy into kinetic. Gears jolting into action, I am immersed in the cacophony of New York City's morning rush-hour traffic.

What may look like chaos to others is, for me, a daily bike commuter, akin to being part of a tightly synchronized symphony. The total concentration required to pedal a bicycle alongside speeding vehicles enters me into an intermediate space—a third space—between my home and my school.

Some may liken the space and state of mind I inhabit during my daily commute to flow. Instead, I prefer to see it as my therapy. My moment of Zen. My "me time" and a routine I cherish.

Reaching bike-friendly Riverside Park, which runs along the perimeter of Manhattan, I see birds flit among the gnarled and peeling camouflage-colored trunks of London plane trees. Here, I am transported to a time and place where I can envision my childhood memories most clearly. Therein, I am a young boy riding alongside a creek in upstate New York. The woods I once frequented now cleared in the name of development. I am in a definitively altered landscape. Before long, I emerge from my blissful past and this tiny oasis of green and cross a hulking metal viaduct. On my left is the Hudson River— the banks of New Jersey further afield. On my right, a set of gleaming yet soulless glass towers. The dualities of the natural and developed worlds clash frequently in urban places, with the latter winning out more often but not always.

My thoughts wander as I cruise by Riverbank State Park and the wastewater treatment plant it sits atop. Sometimes, I think of the network of sewers that snake quietly beneath the city streets. An essential pipeline whose ceaseless flow and terminus feature prominently within the high school environmental science course I teach.

More frequently, I think of the fight local residents successfully won to stop the stench that wafted from the sewage plant into the surrounding neighborhood. The civil disobedience–infused community effort to address the concern had attracted the attention of an environmental litigation firm and, together, in the name of environmental justice, they forced the city to clean up the emissions and cap the wastewater plant with a park. This unlikely partnership is not too dissimilar from those I foster and draw upon in my public school classroom. Partnering with experts creates synergy, redefining what is possible and demonstrating to students how their learning connects to the real world.

Past the park, the green-brown waters of the Hudson return to view. This estuarine section of the river is heavily influenced by the ebb and flow of the tides. In years past, the Lenape called it the Shatemuc, or "the river that flows both ways." These same peoples, known for living in harmony with the land they inhabited, reaped an endless bounty from the Hudson's waters. Perhaps no organism playing a more prominent role than the mighty oyster. *Crassostrea virginica*. A keystone species. An ecosystem engineer. A vitally important organism all but eliminated from the waters I look upon now. Their recent reintroduction to New York waterways—as we shall learn together with my students—offers pathways for renewal and a lesson in hope.

Exploring New York's waters and examining them closely during excursions helps my city-dwelling students shift their gaze—diverting it from the tunnel vision we are all prone to—deepening their connection to and appreciation of nature. And while it is still possible to reconnect and learn from the local environment even in the most urban of places, it is also worthwhile to travel further afield. An annual class trip to the Catskill Mountains, for example, to marvel and learn about our city's water supply firsthand has the capacity to expand students' thinking and horizons.

As I continue to ride, I think of all these things—a sense of place, a connection to the past, a respite from the city, a hope for the future. These ideas lead me, an environmental science teacher whose classroom is in the most urban of settings and who is always looking for authentic and meaningful ways to make learning come to life, to wonder, "How do I connect my students to the real and natural world?"

This question further drives my impetus to break free from the silos of science-specific curriculum and seek opportunities for interdisciplinary connections. Science combined with history, art, mathematics, music, media, and English. Collaborations with colleagues within and across disciplines. Drivers of curriculum and shapers of learning environments.

I continue to pedal toward the George Washington Bridge—its span anchored deep into the bedrock. I take in the vista. The bridge—a symbol of industrial might—and the river flowing below, its contours shaped by an eras-long geological process. The juxtaposition offers yet another reminder of nature's clash with the will of humankind.

My mind continues to meander. How much do the passengers driving along the bridge's span in an endless stream of vehicles know about the even larger volume of water that skirts below them? How do we balance the competing demands of human interest and the natural world? What does a more sustainable future entail? What role should we play in the efforts to better our environment? These questions and many more create guardrails and guidance in my classroom.

Across the river are the Palisades, sheer cliff faces exposed by the last ice age's glacial retreat. The view I see now is like the one Henry Hudson and his crew aboard the *Half Moon* would have witnessed when they sailed these waters over four hundred years ago in search of an elusive northwest passage. The preservation of this vista, however, was far from certain. During the late nineteenth and early twentieth centuries, the igneous diabase rocks of the Palisades were quarried to feed New York's building boom. As rocks disappeared and landscapes were altered, some of the country's first conservationists arrived on the scene. Through a combination of women-led grassroots efforts and monetary backing from industry titans, including the Rockefellers and J. P. Morgan, public and private interests intertwined to persuade the states of New York and New Jersey to designate the Palisades as a park.[1]

This galvanization for the good of green space reminds me of the environmental efforts my students are a part of today. What is their ongoing extracurricular activity and partnership-supported dream? To reimagine the blocks outside their school as an open and accessible pedestrian plaza called the Clean Air Green Corridor, connecting their school and the entire community to a local park. To this day, the call for this urgently needed plan to be fully realized grows larger and closer to fruition than I (and the students) could have ever imagined. The entire effort speaks to the power of young people to advocate for and enact positive environmental change in their own community, representing everything I've ever tried to accomplish with students in and outside the classroom.

Turning right at 155th Street, I leave views of the Hudson behind. The street grid takes hold.

I press harder on my pedals to crest the incline toward Broadway. I enter the Latin pulse that is upper Manhattan. More climbing in the saddle leads me past the Presbyterian Hospital, the one my father's cousin calls the "E.R. in the D.R."—a reference to the large number of Dominican families in this part of the city. Washington Heights—a vibrant cultural exuberance of sights, scenes, flavors, and culture. A place where bachata music blares from welcoming bodegas, sidewalk vendors hawk their wares, and preachers evangelize to the passersby from street-corner pulpits.

In the early morning hours of my commute, however, Washington Heights is more subdued, its troubles more easily observed. As I bear right onto St. Nicholas Avenue, a group of unhoused men gather in a small, triangular-shaped pocket park, awakening from a night spent sleeping in the cold. These men and their living conditions illustrate just one of the many struggles of living in uptown Manhattan. Soaring housing prices and an ever-gentrifying neighborhood have displaced longtime residents. Cruelly and quite paradoxically, the raging opioid and fentanyl drug epidemic plagues those who remain.

My students and their families have not been immune to the increased cost of living. Some who once lived only a short walk away from school now must commute from much further afield—the Bronx, Harlem, and even New Jersey. In class, we learn that their displacement did not happen by chance but instead was connected to intentionally planned policies. We don't avoid these uncomfortable truths. We confront them and explore them deeply, learning how one's environment has been and continues to be shaped by racism and discrimination.

Families hustle children through crosswalks and around street corners. Excitedly looking for my students, I leisurely cruise these last few blocks near my school, eventually passing over the sunken vehicular sewer that is the Trans-Manhattan I-95 Expressway. This blighted highway, one of the busiest in the world, slowly shuttles suburban commuters and delivery trucks directly through Washington Heights, leaving behind a never-ending wall of sound and noxious fumes that contribute to the poor air quality and high asthma rates recorded in this part of the city.[2] Environmental conditions like these and their adverse impacts are just a few of the many environmental injustices faced by the Black and Brown working-class immigrant community that comprises much of the neighborhood. Undoubtedly, it is also a topic of study featured prominently in our science classroom.

The sweet smells of fresh bread and *bizcochos* from the Dominican bakery waft into my olfactory cells. A line of hungry customers wait patiently for their breakfast. On mornings when I have a few extra minutes, I'll stop and grab a bite that I'll later scarf down at my desk during a preparation period. During this brief respite from the ongoing frenzy that is teaching, I'll eagerly rip and then dip a piece of sweet bread into the gooey soup-like oatmeal that is *avena*, washing it down with a blast of rocket fuel–grade café con leche. The rush of sugar and caffeine into my circulatory system is immediate, and for the next few hours, I'll meet (and sometimes beat) the ever-amped energy of my teenage students.

As I cruise around the corner, my school's building comes into view. I hear the excited chatter of children reconnecting with friends on the sidewalk as they await the start of the day. Teachers weave quickly between student groups, hustling toward the front door. Custodians sweep away litter. Yellow school buses and cars drop off more and more students onto the already packed concrete.

Having successfully navigated the crowds, I now climb three flights of stairs, traverse the long hallway leading to my twelfth-grade environmental science classroom, unlock the door, and stash my bike in its designated corner. My trusty steed now stowed, I take in the temporary silence of the spacious corner room I've adorned with posters of the local environment, class pictures of students engaging in fieldwork, exemplary student work, a plethora of air-purifying potted plants, and two turtles rescued from the city's streets.

There is not much time now. I must prepare for the teaching, meetings, grading, consulting, counseling, planning, and advising the day will require. Yes, this is teaching—the nearly impossible profession.

Anxiously awaiting the arrival of the day's first students, I write the lesson objectives and agenda on the board. Throughout the year, we have been learning that the study of one's environment does not have to happen in a textbook reporting on something a world away. Instead, learning about our environment can happen right here, in our city, on the streets surrounding our school.

Learning about our environment in this manner alters our learning environment. We come to understand that the knowledge we already have about where we're from is deepened by getting outside, critically examining history, becoming community scientists, and partnering with local experts to empower and equip us with the knowledge and skills to advocate for change in the name of environmental justice. Our projects teach us that what we learn about and within our environment should be shared and celebrated. Doing so allows us to influence and shape our community for the better. Viewing our world in this localized way redefines the place where we live as not just representative of where we are from but as a shaper of who we are and a determinant of where we will go and may one day yet become.

The school doors are open now. I can hear students shuffling up the stairs. It's time for me to teach and for us to explore how learning about one's environment cannot, nor ever should, be contained by a book's binding or the walls of a classroom.

Author's Note

The preceding retelling of the journey of my commute and preparation for a day in the classroom is an idealized version of teaching and learning. I say as much to recognize the reality that the day-to-day challenges faced by those of us who have ever taught or teach currently are anything but. Indeed, one could argue that the educational landscape today, beset by student behavior and mental health concerns, the uncertainty wrought by the rise of AI, chronic absenteeism, excessive social media use, school shootings and violence, teacher attrition and shortages, and the lingering impacts of the COVID-19 pandemic, are signals of a system in crisis.

However, when I left the classroom following the 2021–22 school year to move to a new city in support of the career journey of my partner, I was not thinking about the challenges across the educational system but instead focused on how I could capture the impossibly messy and incredibly beautiful profession of teaching that I had been practicing for nearly two decades and was about to leave behind. I loved and continue to love teaching about science and the environment; however, I also knew that when I left New York City and its public school system, I would also be leaving the classroom for the foreseeable future and, perhaps, indefinitely.

This decision, partially outside of my control but also one I made intentionally, was influenced by two things. First, the stress of teaching throughout the COVID-19 pandemic in a school community that was disproportionately impacted by the disease had taken a toll on my mental and physical health. While I acknowledge that my ability to leave behind the classroom and the low-income community I served places me in a particularly privileged position, I also hope that by writing this book, I can continue to work in partnership with my former students and colleagues. Indeed, this book is an homage to the students I taught and colleagues I served alongside. Undoubtedly, it is because of them that I can now share with you the actions, approaches, and stories featured in each chapter of this book.

Second, I intuited that the demands of my partner's new job (high school principal) and the impact a move to a new city and school would have on our young family would be great. This possible (and actualized) reality made starting over in a new classroom, in a new school, in a new district, with new systems and structures feel daunting. And while stepping away from the classroom riddled me with guilt as I felt I was leaving my students and, even more so, my colleagues high and dry, the prospect of being able to focus on my family and the aspects of teaching I enjoyed most—helping inspire and create authentic, engaging, and high-quality curriculum at the intersection of science, the environment, and social justice—was exciting.

Now, multiple years separate me from the impact of these two realities and my resulting decision to leave the day-to-day grind that can often be the life of a teacher. This means that the actions, approaches, and stories I share in this book are at risk of being dated and, perhaps more dangerously, told through the rose-colored glasses of a nostalgic. I share as much to recognize and acknowledge this possibility as well as my belief that the most impactful ideas on how to be an effective teacher have been and will always originate on the front lines of the classroom, where the urgency to meet the needs of one's students demands that educators innovate and iterate. Indeed, the foundation of this book is built upon my ongoing attempts in my science classroom to meet my students where they were and construct a learning environment that allowed them to not only gain knowledge and skills but also connect with the world around them. So, while I must recognize that the ever-changing needs of students will and should always inspire and inform new actions and approaches that may be different from those detailed in this book, I nonetheless know from firsthand experience that those I do share have already had and hopefully will continue to have a positive effect on the lives of teachers, students, and the community of which they are a part.

Each chapter of this book is centered on a problem I or my students faced and is accompanied by practical strategies and a contextualized narrative about how that problem was overcome in my environmental science classroom. I recognize that your teaching context may not ask students to hike mountain trails, identify and measure the trees around your school, collect and analyze water samples, create model oyster reefs, use ArcGIS mapping systems, design environmental justice projects, peer into the depths of the sewer system, get their hands dirty in the park across the street, collect food scraps for composting, or advocate for more people to drink water from the tap. However, I am optimistic that the pedagogical approaches and curricular frameworks that were the drivers of these scientific endeavors and environmental actions will. Each approach and accompanying narrative of its application is the result of a yearslong, iterative curriculum-building process fueled by my desire to confront environmental (and educational) injustice and equip my students with the knowledge and skills that could empower them to effect meaningful change in their own community.

Whether it be a new discussion protocol or thinking routine, an overarching framework for field trips, a demonstration of the synergy created by working with experts, the vital elements of cultivating partnerships, a strategy for designing scientific fieldwork opportunities for students, the essential components of hosting a student expo, the impetus for pursuing professional development, ideas for localized learning, or the reminder to celebrate success, it is my sincere belief there is something for every educator within this book—regardless of where they are or who they teach.

Finally, a bit about the structure and how to read this text. This book was written as a narrative and meant to be read sequentially. However, it is also intended to serve concurrently as an actionable guidebook. You are certainly permitted and even welcome to bounce around the text. In your initial read (especially if you're a busy educator), the structure of this text may cause you to inadvertently overlook the actions and approaches featured in these pages. That is why I have included appendices detailing all the strategies included in each chapter, which I hope will help you better utilize this text both now and in the future.

CHAPTER 1

Field Trips, Localized Learning, and Students as Scientists

A Professional Development Journey

The year is 2005. My first in the classroom. The summer's lingering heat that made my un-air-conditioned eighth- and ninth-grade science classroom on the top floor of my school in the Morrisania neighborhood of the South Bronx unbearable has been replaced by cooler, almost crisp air. The arrival of fall temperatures has also chilled the proverbial "honeymoon phase" of a new school year for students and teacher alike. Of late, my naivete and inability to effectively engage my students in the learning process has been on full display. The weight of being responsible for the education of someone else's child—a child most likely to be multiple grade levels behind because of an unjust and inequitable education system—weighs heavily upon my twenty-four-year-old shoulders.

An uncomfortable, almost sinking feeling in my stomach has replaced that mix of energy, idealism, and optimism I felt as a first-year teacher. It has become apparent that my teaching practice needs to change to fully support my students' demands and my expectations. However, because I am only a few months into my nascent career, I don't have the experience, support, or time to meet them.

I take the plastic laminate sheet I had prepared for my class out of its protective binder—the audible "click" of its three rings snapping open and then closed. Laminate sheet in hand, I slide it carefully onto the slick transparent surface of the overhead projector, making sure not to smudge the easily erasable ink and detailed notes prepared upon it.

With a separate blank sheet of paper, I cover all but a few lines of the notes, having learned from experience that if I display too many at once, my students will finish copying them sooner than I am prepared. When satisfied with the setup, I flick the projector switch to "on," immediately illuminating and magnifying the selected lines onto the makeshift projector screen I have fashioned out of four large pieces of overlapping chart paper taped to the chalkboard behind me.

These days, when the daily notes appear, I hear my students' now familiar audible sighs and groans. Despite their protests, however, I ask them, yet again, to copy the notes in preparation for the upcoming test. While many do, I can't help but notice the few who slide their heads slowly toward their desk, comfortably nestling their crown into the crook of their elbow.

I deliver lessons this way because it was how I was taught. The amount of material I feel I need to "cover" in the secondary life science course I teach entails a cornucopia of content a mile wide and an inch deep. The breadth of knowledge that my students will be tested on at the end of the school year compels me, day after day, to dump definitions and terms onto the chart paper display. The responsibility I feel to prepare my students for a test with graduation implications is anxiety inducing. Each class period seems disorderly and never long enough. Some students turn obstinate, and I can no longer coax nor cajole them to copy yet another biological concept into their notebook. Some ceaselessly yearn for hallway-pass escapes from class—breaks from what I retrospectively see was not actually doing science; it was studying the history of it. It has become apparent that something in my pedagogy must change.

Thankfully, the state-mandated science course I teach requires that students engage in several lab activities each year. Sometimes, I must deviate from the note-taking lessons so central to my classroom practice and ask students to engage in a hands-on science lab.

Despite my best preparations and intentions on lab day, however, my classroom often turns chaotic. Inevitably, lab materials fly across the room and those students who are focused on the activity become frustrated by my inability to support them appropriately. In addition to lost materials, there is lost time, meaning many students do not finish the lab they have started, adding fuel to their already simmering frustration.

However, as chaotic and time-intensive as these lab experiences are, I see that students love hands-on activities—providing me with my first clear signal of how important the discovery process is when attempting to engage students in the science classroom. As my turbulent first year in the classroom progresses, I soon come to relish lab day and begin to wonder what other learning adventures are worth pursuing. Maybe there are additional ways to leave note-taking behind and encourage my students to see themselves as scientists. Maybe going outside the classroom, where students can learn from and within the city they live, is a worthwhile venture. Perhaps, I think, it is time for some field trips.

Localized Learning: Field Trip Basics

The first images that come to mind when I think of science field trips are those from *The Magic School Bus* books of my childhood. In these adventurous tales, the zany Ms. Frizzle and her students would leave their classroom and be transported and transformed by their school bus, emerging as scientific professionals immersed in the world of what they were learning.

As a young and proud science nerd, I often imagined myself as one of Ms. Frizzle's students. Whether we were diving to the depths of the ocean floor, zooming around as microscopic investigators inside the human body, or whizzing through space examining stellar objects in the solar system, Ms. Frizzle and her class were always actively practicing science. And now, as a teacher, I was allowed to live out my magic school bus childhood dreams.

The first science trip I arranged for my class (on a yellow school bus) was to the American Museum of Natural History, a world-famous institution that I soon learned my native New York City students had visited every year they had been in school. Consequently, the trip did not live up to my hopes for recreating Ms. Frizzle–like worlds of wonder. Although students did view a cool IMAX movie and visit some interesting exhibit halls during our field trip adventure, their general lack of enthusiasm signaled that better trip planning was necessary to maximize their learning (and engagement).

From then on, I ensured I was better prepared whenever I took my students outside the classroom. To do so, I would always make a point of "pre-visiting" the exhibit or engaging in the experience before my students did. Whenever I could, I would take advantage of the educator evenings that many museums and organizations host. During these professional development events, I would scrutinize an exhibit for instances of the content and skills I was trying to teach my students in class. Taking copious notes as I toured the exhibit hall, I would return home and craft a trip packet that my students would complete when we visited a few weeks later.

The field trip packets mimicked a scavenger hunt, and upon entering an exhibition hall, students would have to utilize the artifacts and information placards in the museum to sketch drawings, complete graphic organizers, and fill in the blanks of fact-filled sentences. My new approach to field trip design had mixed results. For starters, museum docents often complimented me about how conscientious and hard-working my students were. Indeed, many of them worked furiously to complete their packets and looked quite professional holding the wooden clipboards provided to them. We no longer wandered around the museum without purpose, as the packets I produced were robust and kept students busy for the entirety of our visit. Back in the classroom, we would review the answers to the packet—students being sure to fill in any blanks they may have missed—and then turn in their work for a completion grade before we moved on to our next topic of study.

These out-of-school ventures were moderately successful in reinforcing and extending what the students learned in the classroom, so I continued organizing trips this way for several years. I used the pre-trip preparation and post-trip classroom debrief practice to make my students' learning as engaging and meaningful as possible. While students enjoyed escaping the classroom for a day and were learning on each visit, I suspected that something more could be gained from our beyond-the-classroom adventures. In reality, my newly adopted field trip approach was little more than busy work and too similar to the uninspiring practice of note-taking via overhead projector I was still employing, but gradually moving away from, back in the classroom. As difficult as it was to acknowledge this fact, doing so eventually led me to seek out new trip-planning best practices that I hoped would allow my students to become the burgeoning scientists I saw them start to embody during our lab periods.

Unfortunately, being a new teacher in a small, recently established, and under-resourced urban school made finding and embracing new field trip approaches difficult. Compounding these challenges was the lack of experienced science teachers in my school who could have otherwise taken me under their wing and guided me during my first few years attempting to take students outside the classroom. While I did receive guidance from a district-assigned mentor and my teacher preparation program adviser, their support was too infrequent and lacking in the day-to-day contextual understanding of what was happening on the ground in the halls of my school and within the walls of my classroom. As a result, I couldn't shake the feeling that my support system, while well intentioned and of some utility, was incapable of providing me with the ideas and resources I needed to support the students in my classroom. If I wanted to meet my students' needs and provide them with opportunities outside the classroom that would turn them into scientists, I would have to seek out and pursue additional professional learning.

Pursuing Professional Development

The teacher professional development (PD) enthusiast is a unique breed of educator. For one, they are always searching for programs that will allow them to better their craft and, consequently, their ability to provide their students with the best learning experiences possible. They also tend to be willing to spend an inordinate amount of time discussing, thinking, and working to improve their classroom practices. At the same time, the very real need for teachers to improve their practice in service of their students is too often given little more than lip service. In truth, pursuing professional development takes more time and resources than what many already busy and financially burdened educators and school systems have. However, early in my teaching career, I was fortunate enough to have both time (I was dating my future wife, but with no children) and funding (there always seems to be a plethora of PD programming for science, technology, engineering, and math—or STEM—educators to pursue). This reality, in tandem with a mountain of firsthand evidence indicating that my classroom practices needed improvement, allowed me to seek out and then embark on a journey of professional learning that helped me become a better teacher and, consequently, better positioned to support my students both in and outside of the classroom.

Many of the programs sought after by PD enthusiasts occur in the summer. Often, they are associated with places of higher learning such as universities, science-focused charitable foundations, and museums or other large institutions. Collectively, this network recognizes that educators need additional time and space outside of the regular school day and year to fully immerse themselves in professional learning to hone their craft. This fact seemed particularly essential for educators like me who were at the beginning of their careers and tasked with teaching marginalized youth traditionally underrepresented in STEM.

The most attractive professional development programs for teachers are typically free or, in a PD enthusiast's best-case scenario, offer either a stipend, materials for their classroom, an accreditation, or all three. To get accepted into these more prestigious programs, which can vary in length from a weeklong intensive to a whole-summer-long experience, teachers typically need to put together an application, potentially sit for an interview, and likely attend the program during a part or all of their summer break. This last requirement, giving up one's hard-earned and well-deserved summer, is a deal-breaker for a lot of teachers, especially and understandably so for those with young families, but for me, at least when I first started my teaching career unattached and unburdened by a full spectrum of responsibilities, I sought out and participated in as many summer PD programs as possible.

During my first few summers as a teacher, I participated in the lab of an environmental science professor, a college's genetics department, and two other experiences that directly transformed my approach to field trips. The first occurred at the same museum, the American Museum of Natural History, where I often liked to take my students; the second took place in Baltimore over the summer, during which I transitioned from my original school in the Bronx to a new school in northern Manhattan.

A Week at the Museum

The American Museum of Natural History (AMNH) is an institution in every sense of the word and is world-renowned for its collection of artifacts and specimens. Millions of people visit its halls yearly, and its ever-rotating collection of exhibits, films, and items on display is truly magnificent. Aside from its public-facing visage, the museum also has a robust educational program for teachers, including daylong PD workshops, educator evenings, a graduate school of education, and summer programs like the Teacher Renewal for Urban Science Teachers (TRUST) that I was fortunate enough to participate in.

The TRUST program, led by the museum's education staff, shared best practices for using the museum as a learning tool for students. I was among a dozen teachers in the summer PD group. A bonus of our participation in the program included membership to the museum as well as a behind-the-scenes look at its collection (the majority of which, including the museum's actual dinosaur fossils, are never on display and instead used for research by its on-staff scientists). During one particularly memorable tour led by an ichthyologist, our PD group was brought into a cavernous storage room full of rows of tall metal shelves. Upon each shelf were dozens of tightly sealed, preservation fluid–filled glass containers of varying size holding every species of fish imaginable.

During our storage room tour, I distinctly remember seeing a gray metal chest nestled at the base of one of the rows of shelving. It was here that our ichthyologist guide had us gather, slowly opening the chest's lid to reveal a rare specimen of coelacanth, a dinosaur-era "living fossil" of a fish once thought to be extinct until found seren-dipitously by a scientist in a fish market. Learning about this story of rediscovery from our museum expert and seeing a coelacanth with my own eyes solidified my belief that out-of-school experiences for teachers (and students) were worthwhile ventures and inspired me to want to leverage these types of experiences for the classroom.

Indeed, coming face-to-face with an organism once thought to be extinct was a moment that I continue to remember vividly to this day, both for the shock from learning of its existence (I had never heard of a coelacanth) and the spark it reignited by making my childhood magic school bus dreams of learning outside the classroom come to life. In fact, unbeknownst to me as I stood staring into the depths of the coelacanth-holding storage chest, I would, a few years later, go on to make the learning that takes place in informal settings such as science museums the central focus of my thesis as a doctoral student, giving credence to my belief that every educator should pursue their own professional learning journey, as it may benefit or inspire them in unexpected ways.

The Three Phases of Field Trip Planning

Throughout the remainder of the TRUST experience, the museum educators shared research-based best practices and a framework for designing and carrying out field trips. They taught our PD group that a trip was made of three distinct components—pre-trip, during-trip, and post-trip—sharing that neglecting to enact any of these pieces would make an out-of-school experience less meaningful for students.

Pre-trip Phase: Content, Context, and Skills

In my classroom, I thought of the first component of this framework in terms of providing content, context, and skills. Meaning, before any trip, I had to ensure that my students had the background knowl-edge that would allow them to fully engage in the content they might encounter outside the classroom. For example, when taking my stu-dents to the museum's Hall of Human Origins, where they would come face-to-face with their proto-human ancestors, I ensured they had a baseline understanding of what evolution was and how genetics played a part in the evolution of a species over time. Neglecting to do so (as I sometimes did in the earlier parts of my teaching career) would mean preventing my students from fully maximizing their learning, because they would be spending too much time trying to decipher new vocabulary words or evolutionary concepts instead of making connections and extending their knowledge on what they were learning in the classroom.

Providing context during pre-trip preparation was fundamentally related to the content my students were learning but also included an additional big-picture view. For the human origins exhibit, this meant that before any trip, I made my students explicitly aware of where they were going and how what they were learning fit into the broader and overarching unit of study—in this case, genetics and evolution—that we were covering in the classroom. This contextualization would not only help give meaning to our planned excursion but also answer the question that would often arise: "Why are we going on yet another trip to the American Museum of Natural History?"

The final piece of my pre-trip planning focused on the skills my students would need to successfully carry out whatever I asked them to do, on any adventure away from school. And while the skills necessary for a trip to a museum exhibit were basic and not quite applicable to the example I am providing here (besides the skill of completing a handout or packet in an exhibit hall, for which I would suggest letting the students view those materials ahead of time), it is nonetheless not hard to imagine how students, in anticipation of a trip where they were expected to collect data, sketch a drawing, or take photographs, would benefit from having the opportunity to practice in the controlled and calm confines of a classroom.

Providing students with a skill-preparation opportunity (a more appropriate example of which I will detail later in this chapter) would give them both the experience and confidence to successfully carry out what they were expected to do on any given trip. In turn, this skills practice would improve the quality of the work students completed during the trip, free me to spend less time troubleshooting data-collection methods, and increase my availability to help students make connections to the content studied in the classroom.

During-Trip Phase

Instead of telling our PD group what to do for the "during-trip" portion of an excursion, museum educators allowed us to learn through direct participation. During our intentional and engaging wanders in and out of the museum, I realized I was having a lot of fun, and that this essential ingredient was missing from the learning-by-packet out-of-school learning experiences I was currently employing. Nothing solidified this belief more than an experience I thought was impossible in the confines of New York City—canoeing on the Bronx River.

Before our canoe trip, museum educators activated our schema (preexisting background knowledge) by showing our group a short documentary about the ongoing efforts to restore the Bronx River, a blighted but slowly improving waterway. Through the video, we learned of the efforts of scientists and a network of river-focused and like-minded nonprofits working under the umbrella of the Bronx River Alliance to study the history of and help restore this once pristine and vital waterway. We learned how the study of historical maps could help inform the types of native plantings that should take place during riverbank restoration efforts and how the reintroduction of the once-native alewife, a species of fish extirpated from the Bronx River during industrial times, could help rebalance a severely disrupted urban-river ecosystem.

Following our building of background knowledge, our entire PD group spent a whole day outside the museum canoeing and exploring the Bronx River's length. Canoeing on the river provided a visceral firsthand experience of what we had learned in our museum classroom.

The novel and rich experience of paddling a canoe through the heart of the Bronx, a borough better—and unfairly—known for its troubles, was informative and inspirational. Over the course of our paddle, we wove through the old-growth forest contained within the New York Botanical Garden and the Bronx Zoo, portaged over alewife-extirpating industrial-era dams, and floated alongside recently restored riverbanks with long strands of spartina grass gently rustling in the breeze. This experience of doing something in the natural world, in the most urban of places, cemented in my mind that trips can and must aspire to have equal doses of educational content and euphoric celebrations of joy.

Post-trip Phase

For the final component of a successful trip, museum educators emphasized that reviewing what took place during any given outing upon returning to the classroom was essential. However, it was not until I transitioned after six years of teaching in the Bronx to a new school guided by expeditionary learning best practices in northern Manhattan that I truly understood how to fully integrate what happened on a trip into what students were learning in the classroom.

Over the summer that I transferred to my new school, I had the opportunity to participate in a weeklong professional development institute facilitated by the nonprofit EL Education. EL, which stands for "expeditionary learning," is a pedagogical approach that embraces the idea that students learn best by doing. In contrast to my first school, which followed a more traditional teaching model where each class and classroom operated as an isolated and independent unit, EL schools adopt a more interdisciplinary lens. For example, instead of asking students to take notes and then study for a test, EL schools center curriculum on "learning expeditions." In this approach, teachers create learning environments for students that encourage them to learn content and acquire skills through examining case studies, becoming (and interacting with) experts, engaging in hands-on projects, conducting fieldwork (collecting data), and celebrating what they know by sharing it with an authentic (often public) audience. However, at the time that I entered the EL summer institute, I was relatively unfamiliar with what expeditionary learning was and how to incorporate it into my teaching practice. Thankfully, the institute, which was hosted in Baltimore's charming Inner Harbor, was led by EL's educator-experts.

During the week of professional learning, my group actively participated in an expedition that focused on the threatened health of the Chesapeake Bay, a natural wonder and essential economic engine of the Mid-Atlantic. As I was learning about the Chesapeake, I realized the power of embracing out-of-school trips as opportunities to engage in fieldwork—a tenet of EL curriculum design. According to EL, trips out of the classroom should not be viewed as isolated learning experiences but instead as fieldwork opportunities for students to collect and then analyze data upon returning to the classroom. In this manner, students act as a scientist, sociologist, or any other researcher in a particular field of expertise investigating the answer to a question or solution to a problem.

At the EL summer institute, this meant that my PD group had to determine the health of the Chesapeake Bay by collecting water samples from Baltimore's Inner Harbor, examining the impacts of a local stormwater waste collection system and celebrity dubbed Mr. Trash Wheel, speaking with local scientists, and visiting a blue crab research station. Collectively, these fieldwork experiences (which also happened to be quite joyful) and the data we analyzed in regard to the health of the Chesapeake Bay in our teacher's classroom forever transformed my view of what trips could be and how students should learn outside of school.

A New Approach to Field Trips

That fall, after my EL summer institute experience, I was in a new school, teaching environmental science to high school seniors and excited to put all that I had learned about how to craft, carry out, and learn from trips into place. It is also why, in what was only the second week of school, seventy-five or so of my students from three different class sections were crammed into my classroom, ready to depart for a day of fieldwork on the Bronx River.

Before our trip day, I had made sure to activate my students' background knowledge by designing lessons about estuaries and water quality and contextualizing our trip within our unit on the restoration of the Bronx River. We learned the characteristics of an estuary (influenced by tides and made of brackish water) and how New York City's waterways were a mighty confluence of freshwater rivers and the salty Atlantic Ocean. We also viewed the same AMNH Bronx River restoration video that I had seen at TRUST and learned how the river we would soon visit was turning from a cesspool of industrial waste into a slowly improving waterway.

I also trained my students on the water quality testing skills they would need to complete fieldwork during our visit to the river. To practice, I provided them with the same test kits for dissolved oxygen (a molecule essential for aquatic organisms' survival and one often used as a de facto measurement of water quality), pH, turbidity (water clarity), temperature, and salinity that we would use at the river and spent an entire class period letting them carry out each test using tap water from the lab sinks in our classroom.

Students as Scientists: Writing Claims, Supported by Evidence and Reasoning

The other skill that I wanted my students to practice before our trip was determining the survivorship of the aquatic organisms one might find in an estuary. During this skill practice, I asked students to learn about the limits of tolerance needed for the survival of estuarine organisms like crabs, oysters, and alewives and, using a fictitious water quality data set, determine whether each species could survive under those conditions. Students compared the tolerable ranges of temperature, dissolved oxygen, pH, and other water quality parameters required by each species to the data set I provided. Next, they synthesized a claim supported by evidence and reasoning on whether each species they were studying could or could not survive given the water quality conditions. This activity, which aligned with Next Generation Science Standards (NGSS) and had students "engaging in argumentation," was based on the "claim, evidence, reasoning scientific explanation" framework developed by education researchers at the University of Michigan, and helped me diagnose a student's ability to think and write like a scientist.[1]

Each part of the scientific explanation framework mimics the approach of scientists. First, scientists must craft a research question—the driver of the discovery process. For my students, the question I provided was, "Will organism—alewife, oyster, etc.—(a) just survive, (b) survive and reproduce, or (c) die, given the current water conditions?" Scientists next craft a hypothesis (for the "limits of tolerance" activity, we called this a "claim") based on prior background knowledge and observed or collected evidence (a.k.a. the fictitious water quality data I provided students). Finally, once scientists have collected sufficient and appropriate evidence, they link the claim and evidence together via reasoning or, more specifically, these components' connection in accordance with a scientific field's body of knowledge. For my students, this meant they needed to explain how the claim they made and the evidence they used to support it correlated with an organism's survivorship within the estuarine conditions provided.

During my students' first attempt at writing like a scientist, which happened in the classroom, I explicitly told them that they would be assessed again on this skill after they had collected their water quality data at the Bronx River. Doing so helped illustrate how practicing the claim-evidence-reasoning approach on a fictitious data set in the classroom was directly connected to what we would be actively carrying out on our trip, thus adding meaning and authenticity to our venture.

Localized Learning: The During-Trip Experience

From my prior experience of taking students out of the classroom, I knew that logistical preparation was essential. This meant that by the time seventy-five students were crowded into my classroom on the morning of our adventure, I had already confirmed the date and time and the activities we would participate in with the Bronx River Alliance (BRA) education staff who would be hosting us at the Bronx River. It also meant I had met with the trip's chaperones—doing a run-through of our day of canoeing, water sampling, seine netting, and crab fishing—assigning each to a group of students. Also planned was our route to the park, consisting of two different subway lines and twenty minutes of walking. And as a final task before departing for the day, I divided all the materials we would need to carry—data-collection handouts, clipboards, pencils, water-sampling kits, crab bait, crab baskets, sunscreen, and more—among student volunteers.

Logistics complete, our group would set out for the park, and after completing a lengthy subway ride, we would clop down the stairs of the subway onto busy Westchester Avenue—walking past auto body repair shops, bodegas, and live poultry slaughterhouses. We would then cross the Sheridan Expressway and slip down a path into a sliver of a park nestled between a subway overpass, the Amtrak Acela train tracks, and a network of local streets. The looming remnants of an old concrete plant that provided the green space we were visiting—the fittingly named Concrete Plant Park—would greet us at the bottom of the path only a few yards from the banks of the Bronx River. At the bottom of the trail, the BRA education staff would wait next to a series of neatly arranged canoes and we'd slowly join them. Once our group had fully arrived, I would look around and smile, feeling confident that the content, context, skills, and pre-trip preparation had set the stage for a science-filled and enjoyable day of fieldwork.

Settling into our fieldwork environs, we would stand in a circle and—mere moments before breaking away into groups for the day's planned activities—I would set the mood and outline expectations. I would ask my students, some already donning their personal flotation devices and gripping a canoe paddle, to take turns reading lines from a poem by Joseph Rodman Drake, a native Bronxite. The first stanza reads:

> I sat me down upon a green bank-side,
> Skirting the smooth edge of a gentle river,
> Whose waters seemed unwillingly to glide,
> Like parting friends who linger while they sever;
> Enforced to go, yet seeming still unready,
> Backward they wind their way in many a wistful eddy.[2]

The purpose of reading Drake's poem was to transport my students back to another time when the Bronx River was a bucolic backwater surrounded by salt marshes and farmland. I wanted them to imagine what the natural environment in this place used to be like and appreciate the restoration efforts they had learned about in the classroom and, as a result, benefited from during their trip experience. Through this activity, I returned to the content and context of what we had been learning in the classroom and connected it to our instructional experience in the field.

After our opening circle activity ended, content and context successfully revisited and extended, student groups would scatter across various learning stations. One group would break off with BRA educators for a quick introduction to canoeing before setting off for an estuary paddle. A second would dip a bucket into the river and begin water sampling. A third would start tying pieces of twine around chicken gizzards, dropping them into the river and hoping to catch some blue crabs, or they would find a quiet place to sit and sketch a drawing of the river and its surroundings. A final group would wriggle into waders before plodding off with seine nets toward the shoreline in pursuit of other aquatic creatures. Confident that all the day's learning components were now in motion, I would then focus on supporting the primary intent of our fieldwork—the assessment of the Bronx River's health.

The first thing one may notice when glancing at the greenish-brown waters of the Bronx River is the abundance of trash floating on the surface. On the days we would visit, various pieces of detritus would often include a plethora of plastic bottles, an assortment of game balls, and many single-use plastic bags. Thankfully, a bright-orange trash boom spanning the river's width kept the floating amalgamation of litter from being swept downstream. Seeing all the debris often made my students question the river's cleanliness and capacity to harbor life. Sometimes, however, looks can be deceiving, and I encouraged my students to do their analysis despite what was observable on the surface.

Because we had practiced using the water test kits back in the classroom, my students knew exactly what to do with them on the banks of the Bronx River. They measured water samples with reagents and testing materials for the same parameters (pH, salinity, dissolved oxygen, temperature) as those measured for a few days before. They approached their work with the seriousness of a field scientist, because I had contextualized their water testing at the river into the broader scope of our estuary unit. Indeed, the students were aware that the results they collected in the field would be analyzed the day after our trip and used for another scientific claim-evidence-reasoning assessment back in the classroom.

After all the students had rotated through the various learning stations for the day, having tons of fun along the way, we regrouped with BRA educators for a closing circle. In these closing moments of the trip, in some ways the most important of the entire day for their potential to solidify all the learning that had taken place in the field, students would often reflect on how their Bronx River experience changed what they knew about estuaries and the borough of the Bronx itself. Oftentimes they would share their surprise at how many living things their seine nets had captured from a river littered with trash and remark on how much fun it was to canoe for the first time. Others would joyfully describe their experience of successfully landing a blue crab in their fishing basket or the precision with which they were able to collect measurements from their water samples. Each story share-out added to the learning the students gained and the fun they experienced, prompting continual requests for more trips throughout the rest of the school year centered on collecting and analyzing data from the local environment (which I gladly accommodated). Finally, after reflections were shared—properly bookending our day's learning—we would gather for a class photo. Turning toward the camera lens, using the Bronx River we had just so thoroughly explored, sketched, and collected data from as our backdrop, we would smile and then depart, taking the same pathway we had embarked on a few hours before, toward the subway and our long return to the school.

Localized Learning: The Post-trip Experience and Reflections on Professional Growth

Back in the classroom, laminate plastic sheets of notes a now long-distant memory, I projected our smile-laden class trip photo on the screen at the front of the room as students entered their water quality data into an online spreadsheet. We calculated water parameter averages and then discussed the results. Students examined patterns and trends, identified outliers, looked for sampling errors, and thought of new opportunities for analysis. I asked students to evaluate the river's health for their final content and skills assessment. Using the data they had just collected, they wrote new claim-evidence-reasoning statements to determine whether the sampled Bronx River water could support the estuarine species they had studied before our trip. Using our class data, each student would come to their own conclusion—demonstrating their ability to write scientific explanations (for the second time) and learning that the Bronx River estuary was more than capable of harboring a variety of life.

A few days later, reading through my students' responses that demonstrated measurable growth compared to our first attempt in the classroom using the claim-evidence-reasoning writing approach, I took a moment to reflect on my journey to get to this point in my teaching practice. I saw how failure and frustration as a new teacher led me toward professional development and improvement in trip planning. My professional learning experiences provided me with not only an actionable framework that I could use to approach and enact out-of-school experiences but also one I could utilize to improve my students' learning experiences and outcomes.

Instrumental to this pathway was first viewing field trips as not just an opportunity to get students outside the classroom (although a noble outcome) but as an intentional way to connect what was happening in the classroom to the world. Additionally, embracing the pre-trip, during-trip, and post-trip framework that the educators at AMNH had taught me was necessary and the driver of ensuring that my students had learned the essential content, context, and skills to maximize their out-of-school learning. Also informative was EL Education's view that field trips should contain fieldwork opportunities for students to collect data from the world around them and act as scientists. Lastly (and perhaps most importantly), ensuring that adventures beyond the classroom were joyful unified all I had learned and experienced through my professional development to improve my students' learning environment. And although the path was long and took me across multiple schools and years, reading the final claim-evidence-reasoning assessments and reflecting with my students after our trip to the Bronx River demonstrated that the time and effort were worth the journey.

But what about educators based in schools or other geographical regions teaching other grades or subject areas? What lessons can be learned from my professional learning journey that can translate to new contexts and content areas? For starters, I would encourage all teachers to take the leap and find one thing that they are truly interested in bringing into their classroom. This could be a new pedagogical approach or subject (maybe even a current hobby) one is particularly passionate about. Indeed, after I shared an early draft of this book with a close colleague, they shared with me that they had recently signed up for a workshop they had previously been putting off. And while it is commendable that my colleague took the initiative to kick-start their own professional learning that may, over time, take them on as powerful a journey as my own, I must also recognize that many educators remain rightfully skeptical of pursuing professional development given the huge demand already placed on their limited time and energy by an overarching and overbearing education system and society.

Even "in-service" days (workdays dedicated to professional learning for faculty and staff while students remain at home) that could serve as opportunities for educators to explore their pedagogical and personal passions are often dominated by mandatory trainings or workshops focused on broader district or school initiatives. Yes, such forms of training are sometimes necessary. However, I suggest that if this is the only professional learning format being provided for teachers, then something is amiss. Indeed, what is omitted from this top-down approach to professional development is the on-the-ground interests of individual teachers. That is why I am and will always be a proponent for educators to pursue professional development experiences that fills their soul, and it's why I ask administrators who are not already facilitating this type of professional learning for their staff to empower educators with the agency of choice, the power of the purse, and, perhaps most importantly, the necessary amount of release time to pursue their passions. Just imagine how teaching and learning might be transformed if each educator, using their vast and deep knowledge of the students they interact with and support each day, was provided with their own professional development budget, with the only expectation being that they utilize it, in full, to learn something new that is pedagogically adjacent to what they are interested in.

While the empowerment I felt and initiative I took to pursue my own professional development meant becoming an expert on how to craft localized learning experiences that added authenticity and rigor to my curriculum—core tenets of my teaching practice that, as we shall see in subsequent chapters, can equip students to enact social change in their own community—other educators' learning journeys may, and should, look different. Perhaps there is a math teacher interested in incorporating gaming into their curriculum, or an English teacher looking to tie standards for argumentation to documentary filmmaking—what would their professional learning journey look like? Chances are the content of the PD courses for those teachers would look different from my own but also contain some elements that are similar. One can expect that deepening their content and pedagogical practices and fully incorporating a new way of teaching into their classroom requires them to evolve over multiple years and iterations. That is why teachers should start small but also be open to thinking big and reimagining the future (a core and repeated suggestion of how to incorporate the actions and approaches presented in this book). Pursue a passion, investigate an interest, explore a hobby. Then, if the professional pursuit has potential, bring it into the classroom. Continue to iterate and follow the professional learning trail. See where it may lead, because who knows, one day a childhood dream like the spell cast by Ms. Frizzle and her magic school bus over her classroom may be conjured into your own reimagined and longed-for learning environment.

CHAPTER 2

The Hook and the Circle

Routines for Student Engagement, Thinking, and Dialogue

With the US surgeon general calling for social media warning labels and the publication of social psychologist Jonathan Haidt's bestselling *The Anxious Generation*, the 2024–25 school appears to be a watershed moment in the now (somewhat) coordinated effort to restrict the usage of cell phones in schools.[1] The confluence of the surgeon general's warning and Haidt's evidence-based (yet contested) argument that connects the collapse of children's (especially girls') mental health to the rise of social media and smartphones has captured the attention of states legislative bodies across the country, leading to a slew of new rules and regulations restricting student cell phone use in schools.

Years before social media and smart phone–related regulations began passing through state legislatures, educators—ever the first responders to the needs and interests of children— were seeing firsthand the challenges wrought by trying to get students to turn their attention away from their phones and engage with the content of a lesson and each other. At the same time, my colleagues and I also saw the benefit of students having access to the proverbial "world at their fingertips" and often tried to leverage their affinity to digital devices by incorporating their usage into classroom assignments and projects. Putting the real benefits of devices in the classroom aside, however, I found that when left to their own accord, many of my students struggled to keep their phones in their pockets when expected to do so.

One of my responses to this ongoing challenge was to incorporate thinking and discussion routines that asked students to look up from the screens in their hands and respond to thought-provoking lesson "hooks" and face-to-face discussion protocols. As almost any teacher will tell you, this incorporation of routines into the classroom adds a familiar structure to the learning environment that students need to succeed. Indeed, I found that once routines became familiar (especially for students whose home lives were chaotic and unpredictable), learning was more readily facilitated because the routines clarified expectations and made the time we spent together more efficient. And while it is certainly possible that too many routines can stifle learning, creativity, and comfort in the classroom, a dearth of predictability makes the creation of a successful learning environment impossible.

The Hook: Mystery Pieces and Thinking Routines

Projected on the screen at the front of the classroom is a group of brightly dressed Ethiopian women and children walking across the desert. Strapped across their backs are large yellow plastic containers known as jerry cans. In the distance are small tufts of scrubland, and the outline of a mountain sits atop the horizon. To activate my students' schema, I ask them to critically examine this "mystery piece," using a popular routine known as "See, Think, Wonder"—one of a series of classroom practices designed by the Harvard Graduate School of Education's Project Zero to help teachers visualize their students' thinking.[2] During the routine, I would ask students, "What do you see in the image?" "What thoughts come to mind as you make your observations?" and "What new ideas or questions do you have as a result of your observations and wonderings?" The mystery piece—an expeditionary learning approach that is designed to hook students—purposefully provides a hint of what will come in an upcoming unit of study and, when used in combination with a thinking routine like

"See, Think, Wonder," can heighten student engagement by eliciting more questions than answers.

During our ensuing discussion, students question where the women are going, ask about the utility of the jerry cans, and wonder why there are no men in the picture. I encourage them to share their thoughts, asking them to build and expand upon each other's ideas.

To further contextualize our conversation and add an additional layer of mystery, we view a short video that flashes photographs of women and children struggling to fill jerry cans with water. The water in the images is visibly dirty and of insufficient supply; its source is an amalgam of muddy holes pocketing otherwise dry riverbeds and quickly emptying cisterns. The stress and strain on the women's faces and bodies are palpable, conveying anxiety-inducing questions of what happens when the water source runs dry. At the video's conclusion, we continue co-constructing our understanding of the original image. Before long, the intent of the "mystery piece" becomes apparent. The women and children we saw in the opening image of the class were on a never-ending journey to collect water for their survival.

After screening the video, I ask my students to estimate their daily water usage. Answers range widely from one gallon a day to a few thousand. The juxtaposition of their answers with the mystery-piece conversation creates the cognitive dissonance I hoped for, priming my students' minds for learning and new understandings of their own city's water supply.

The next activity, which is still a part of our new unit's opening hook, asks each student to more accurately calculate their daily water use. To do so, they must answer myriad questions about their water habits using an online calculator.[3] Survey questions range widely. Do you keep the water running while you brush your teeth? Do you take baths or showers? Do you flush the toilet after every time you urinate? After each response, students can see a daily total water-usage figure being tallied at the bottom of the screen.

Upon the survey's completion, a buzz fills the room. Students share their final water-usage totals as if grades on a major exam had just been released. Echoes of "What'd you get? What'd you get?" are followed by a cacophony of comparisons. Once the chatter dies down, I ask students to input their results into a spreadsheet accessible to the entire class. Thanks to hidden cellular formulas, class averages are instantly revealed. Students compare their totals to their classmates (and mine) and study how their water usage measures against people in different countries, including the Ethiopian women from our mystery-piece image.

I next ask students to reflect on their water consumption estimates from the beginning of class. They realize that their initial estimates of a few gallons to a few thousand gallons of water per day are well off the mark, with actual totals typically settling in the range of 100 to 200 gallons per day. During our conversation, some students, stunned by their water usage, pledged to waste less water. Others share how fortunate they feel to open a tap and be greeted by an endless supply of H_2O. A few even admit to feeling guilty—a normal reaction for teens when discussing environmental issues—to which I relay that this feeling is normal and even okay. During these instances, I also seize the opportunity to ask students to think more deeply—beneath the surface of their results and initial reactions—encouraging them to question how our societal norms and lifestyles compare and contrast with others, helping them foster reflective and empathetic practices.

If my opening hook and thinking routines have succeeded, I have encouraged many of my students to put away their phones and focus on the task at hand. Doing so has allowed them to engage in the mystery of the opening image, activating their schema and contextualizing their learning. Now it is time to capitalize upon this initial engagement and learn more about the Ethiopian women seen in the mystery piece, the villagers of Foro, and a woman named Aylito Binayo. To do so, we turn to reading and discussing the *National Geographic* article "The Burden of Thirst" by Tina Rosenberg.[4] A piece of writing over a decade old, but with a message on world water scarcity that still rings true: access to the world's natural resources remains unequal. To further investigate this unfortunate reality, we use Rosenberg's text to anchor us in our next curricular adventure and facilitate deeper engagement and understanding via dialogue.

The Socratic Circle

Whenever I asked students to read, analyze, and discuss a complex text like "The Burden of Thirst," the Socratic circle was my go-to classroom activity. Sometimes referred to as Socratic seminars or "fishbowls," Socratic circles can be viewed as a framework and approach for supporting reading comprehension and facilitating student-driven conversations. Most of my ideas and inspiration for how and why to use Socratic circles was inspired by educator Matt Copeland's book, *Socratic Circles: Fostering Critical and Creative Thinking in Middle and High School.*[5] While there are many things I took away from Copeland's text that informed my take on Socratic circles, including insights on student and teacher roles, how to prepare students to participate in dialogue, what classroom conversations should look and sound like on discussion day, and ideas on how to assess (if at all) student contributions to the conversation, the central component I gained from the book was a routine for fostering student engagement in the classroom.

Socratic Circle Preparation

On the basis of my classroom experience using Project Zero's visible thinking routines and my reading of Copeland's book, I knew that student-centered conversations had the potential to be compelling learning opportunities. To foster them, I took Socratic circle preparation seriously and set aside at least one class period for students to read and annotate a text, in this case "The Burden of Thirst." The dedication of class time for reading was necessary because not doing so often meant that a portion of my students would come to class on Socratic circle day unprepared, detracting from the learning experience of the class as a whole. While we can debate the merits and pitfalls of using class time for something many educators may view as homework, I knew that if I wanted my students to be prepared to engage in deep and meaningful conversations, I needed to provide them with time to read in class.

While reading in class, students were required to stop every few paragraphs (I would mark in the text where to do so) and construct one-sentence summaries of what they had read. This approach was beneficial because it gave students a quick break from deciphering and decoding complex passages and the opportunity to make sense of what they had just read. While I always encouraged my students to go above and beyond the required target of eight to twelve one-sentence summaries, I found that this simplified approach provided sufficient preparation for Socratic circle discussion day.

To provide structure on reading days, I would break the class into two groups. Strong readers were allowed to work independently and at their own pace at their tables, whereas students identified as struggling readers were pulled to the front of the classroom. In this emerging readers' group (which my stronger readers were always welcomed to join), I (or another student) would read the article aloud, stop at the required one-sentence summary locations, facilitate a short conversation to help our group comprehend the text, and, with student input, help draft one-sentence summaries. This community-centered inclusive reading practice was one that I found to be both helpful in supporting my struggling readers and incredibly beneficial to the overall richness and depth of the conversation students had with each other in the ensuing Socratic circle.

When students finished reading a text and writing their one-sentence summaries, they were expected to engage in one last piece of preparation. This entailed reviewing a dozen questions about the text I had generated and attached to the end of the article. For some students, this meant simply reading them before Socratic circle day. In contrast, others went as far as to write down their answers to each question or even practice what they might say, imagining themselves in our discussion circle. Regardless of which approach students chose, all had access to the questions that would drive the Socratic circle conversation.

The Socratic Circle:
Facilitating Student Conversations

On Socratic circle day, students arrived at a transformed learning environment. At the center of the classroom was a circle of chairs.

Around this central circle, where the main dialogue of the day would occur, was another circle of tables. The shape of these two circles was essential—their lack of corners provided ample and equal opportunity for all participants to be seen and heard by all in attendance.

As students crossed the classroom threshold, I assigned each to either the inner circle of chairs or the outer circle of tables. The group seated in the inner circle was up first for conversation. The second circle, or "gallery," perched on tabletops hovering above their classmates, had been tapped for active listening. The members of this listening group served an essential purpose: their elevated perches allowed them to be both audience members and evaluators. It gave the participants seated below them a feeling not too dissimilar from what athletes might experience competing inside an arena, heightening the experience and level of play.

After a brief welcome and reminder of the rules of engagement—chief among them the expectation for respectful dialogue and our shared pursuit of a deeper understanding of the text we had read and the subject we were studying—I turned the class over to the inner circle. Soon after, a seated student would nominate one of the provided discussion questions for conversation and then respond, sharing their thoughts, ideas, and opinions and referencing their one-sentence summaries as evidence to support their remarks.

As this first student concluded their comments, another student could seamlessly jump in (raising hands was not necessary nor expected), adding their thoughts and ideas. This pattern was repeated, followed by another student and then another. In this manner, the dialogue became a free-flowing discussion among peers, the process beginning again when a new question was raised, surfacing issues of race and poverty central to "The Burden of Thirst" and motivating students to compare the lived experience of Binayo and the villagers of Foro to their own.

After fifteen minutes of conversation in which every single one of my students' voices was often heard (a beautiful sight and sound to behold), it was time for the outer circle—whom I frequently caught biting their tongues, resisting the urge to jump into the conversation—to converse. Using our Socratic circle scoring rubric as a guide, the outer circle provided constructive feedback to their inner-circle classmates before standing up and swapping places, moving from tables to chairs. Then, the former tabletop group, now seated in the inner circle, would follow the same cycle as before: choose a question to start, engage in dialogue, and then shift to a new question. At the same time, their classmates, now comprising the outer circle of listeners and evaluators, would wait patiently for their opportunity to provide feedback.

The Socratic Circle: The Teacher's Role

As soon as the dialogue of a Socratic circle was underway, my role, like the outer circle's, shifted to that of active and silent listener. As difficult as it was to turn the classroom's discourse completely over to my students, I pledged not to provide any commentary unless the conversation became overly contentious, too tangential, or contained egregious factual errors. As a result of my "fly on the wall" stance, I had time to intently listen, take notes, and keep a tally on student participation using a class roster sheet, marking each time a student spoke and typing in a spreadsheet I had open on my laptop what each student had said—verbatim.

Taking notes this way was essential because I would review them after class to assess each student's discussion skills and understanding of the text we had read, using the same scoring rubric that the outer circle was given to shape their feedback during class (and that all students were provided with before Socratic circle day). While there are differing perspectives on whether Socratic circles should be formally assessed, I found that providing each student with a grade increased the rigor and quality of the conversation and incentivized every single one of them to participate.

The first time that students received grades from a Socratic circle, many were surprised that their scores (despite my pre-discussion review of norms and expectations) were not based on the number of times they participated but centered on the content of their dialogue. Sometimes, students scored much lower than they had expected. In the spirit of giving students multiple opportunities to demonstrate their understanding, I always provided the option of submitting revisions in the form of a written response to the questions discussed. In this manner—over an entire school year in which students participated in several Socratic circles, repeatedly engaging in complex and content-rich texts—they refined and honed their reading and discussion skills, demonstrating measurable growth in their abilities (and grades).

Of all the texts we read and Socratic circles we had throughout the year, the first about Binayo and the women of Foro was perhaps the most powerful. The story in "The Burden of Thirst," with its vivid descriptions of the day-to-day life and struggles faced by women in Ethiopia to survive in their environment, in addition to the well-intentioned but flawed attempts by a host of organizations to address them, was supposed to be discussed, not just read.

Many of my students, who inherently understood how vital access to a clean and reliable water source was, were previously unfamiliar with the idea that all of humanity did not share the relative luxury of turning a tap and watching the water flow. Indeed, their reality of unfettered access to fresh and clean water provided the perfect lens for my students to view the subject of our next exploration—their city's drinking water supply.

Bringing the Hook and the Circle to Your Classroom

Hooks, mystery pieces, visible thinking activities, and Socratic circles are all routines. Routines can help make learning for students more engaging and efficient and encourage them to keep their phones in their pockets. Routines can also be adopted, adapted, and shared across various classroom content areas and grade levels. Indeed, a shared expeditionary learning curriculum, working in tandem with "in-house" teacher-designed and -led professional development learning cycles, went a long way at my school toward ensuring that best practices like Socratic circles and visible thinking routines were incorporated across myriad subject areas and grade levels.

In each classroom context, my colleagues added unique twists to each routine to best engage their students and meet their classroom objectives. Want to pique students' interest in the new earth science tectonic plates unit? Use a mystery piece to literally flip the classroom upside down—tip over desks, push tables on their side, and roll out the yellow caution tape—and have students enter the class as if an earthquake had just occurred. Looking to increase students' abilities to interpret and analyze a series of data sets in math class? Use a visible thinking routine (there are dozens) such as See, Think, Wonder to identify background knowledge and possible misconceptions. Want to familiarize students with the multiple perspectives of colonists in the years leading up to the Revolutionary War? Ask them to read and discuss primary sources written by Patriots and Loyalists and discuss the multiple perspectives during a Socratic circle. The point being that routines can provide adaptable structures for use in classroom learning environments that teachers can mold and utilize to encourage students to put down their phones and deepen their class's understanding of a course's content and one another.

CHAPTER 3

An Exploration of New York City's Water Supply

The Pursuit of Passionate Pedagogy

Because I taught an elective, I know that my classroom circumstances were sometimes much different from those faced by other educators, where tests and teacher accountability took precedence over student engagement and deeper learning. I also want to acknowledge the impact that high-stakes standardized testing can have on teachers' lessons and students' learning. Having been a teacher of record for a course that ended in a statewide assessment, I am familiar with the weight and pressure teachers feel when trying to prepare their students for a standardized test—for me, it was immense. Indeed, I was often conflicted when I found myself "teaching to the test": dramatically deviating from my preferred "depth over breadth" approach filled my teacher soul with heavy doses of angst and guilt. Deep down, I did not want to take a test-centric route to lesson planning, but nonetheless felt I had to if I wanted to best prepare my students for an assessment with high school graduation implications.

Politicians, data-driven education reformists, and others too quickly suggest that a good teacher will find a way to do both—dive deep into the subject matter and prepare students for standardized tests. They will make the case that standardized testing is necessary for teacher accountability to measure student "progress" and hold educators accountable. And while I do feel there is value in standardized testing (in particular when implemented to measure growth over time and inform instruction), I must also point out that the pressures a test-centric focus places on educators can have the unintended consequence of creating a top-down, "race to the bottom" learning environment that can suck the joy out of many a classroom and cause us to lose sight of education's true purpose—the cultivation of lifelong learners and an informed and engaged citizenry.

So, what is the answer to countering a test-centric system? How can we recapture the hearts and minds of stressed-out educators and intellectually stunted, bored, and disinterested students? One answer is to encourage teachers to find the space, courage, and support to bring what they are most passionate about into their classroom. For me, that meant teaching my environmental science students about the history and science behind their city's water supply.

A Passionate Thirst for the Natural World

My passion for science and the environment was an outgrowth of the countless hours I spent as a boy exploring the meandering trails and cold-water creek behind the subdivision of my childhood home in upstate New York. One of my earliest memories of interacting with nature is of catching frogs in the stream that ran through the woods at the bottom of a steeply pitched slope in my backyard and corralling them into a child-sized hard-plastic blue swimming pool in my driveway. Placing the frogs into the pool alongside the miniature boats and other floating accoutrements I had arranged for their enjoyment, I would entertain myself and my newfound amphibious friends for days on end until I woke up in the middle of one particularly core-memory-inducing night with the realization that I was not the natural world's friend but its captor. I determinedly made my way to my slumbering parents' bedroom and, much to their displeasure, demanded that we release the amphibians—immediately. The entirety of this experience anchored my connection to nature and seeded my desire to help conserve and protect it.

As a teacher, having long left the bucolic beginnings of my upbringing behind for classroom adventures of the urban variety, I forever searched for ways to reconnect myself and my students with the natural world. And while living and teaching science in a city like New York made environmental escapes more difficult, I found that incorporating my passion for the natural world into the classroom was always worthwhile. Indeed, when I first learned about the up-state watershed that supplied the city of New York with its drinking water—a bounty of protected forested land not too far from where I grew up—I knew I had found a way to connect my lived experience and passion for the environment to the classroom.

When I first learned about New York City's drinking water supply, I was struck by its enormity. The statistics associated with the system are staggering. Every day, over one billion gallons of water is delivered to nearly nine million people via the system's network of controlled dams and reservoirs, which stores up to 550 billion gallons at a time.[1] From its most distant point, drinking water is transported by gravity from over one hundred miles away through some of the longest tunnels in the world and made safe for consumption by water treatment facilities—each an impressive feat of engineering in its own right. In addition, the creation and ongoing development and operation of the system is inextricably linked to the success of the city for which it was built, helping to quell disease, fight fire, and quench the thirst of America's largest urban population. As I learned these facts about New York City's drinking water, the more fascinated I became. The more fascinated I became, the more I knew I had to share my learning with my students. Before long, water seeped into and soon inundated my curriculum, as teaching my students about all things related to New York City water had become a passion project.

As I embarked upon this curricular refashioning, I saw the water in and around New York City as a means to locally contextualize what my students were learning in the classroom and an opportunity to immerse them in a tangible environmental topic. Thankfully, I was able to infuse this topic and its scientific content into my environmental science elective class, where I had much flexibility and freedom to let my hydrological passions drive the course's scope and sequence. And while the curriculum I crafted around New York City's water supply was always informed by the needs and interests of my students, I also felt that the opportunity to teach about a topic I was passionate about heightened the learning experience for all.

But what about teachers without the opportunity to teach an elective and who perhaps are unable to incorporate their unique passions into the curriculum? Perhaps the need to teach a top-down or scripted curriculum makes teaching one's passion complicated or even fraught with risk. In these circumstances, teachers must acknowledge two things. First, your circumstances are challenging; second, you must, despite this unfortunate reality, find the courage to teach your (classroom-content-related) passion anyway. Below, I offer a few ways that will hopefully inspire you to do so.

The Jigsaw + Gallery Walk Routine

To introduce what would turn into an extended exploration of New York City's water supply, I would start by incorporating a new mystery-piece activity. In this instance, I would give each pair of students in my class a sealed envelope. Inside would be an assortment of cards with images that displayed the various components of a water supply system. Pictures on each card ranged from lakes and reservoirs to pipes, faucets, septic tanks, and even a bucket. The directions asked students to arrange the cards on their table to represent how water travels to their faucet and then from their faucet to its final destination.

When given the signal to begin, each pair would tear into their envelope and quickly spread their cards across their desk. A lively and, at times, argumentative discussion would ensue. In these opening moments, I would always encourage a robust debate and rarely (as long as conversations were focused) interrupt a rising volume of voices in the classroom. In this instance, the crescendo of sound, which to the misguided observer would be the mark of a disinterested classroom, indicated that students were engaged and invested in finding a solution to their given task.

Once all the water infrastructure cards were removed from each envelope, they were continually sorted, grouped, and rearranged.

After a few minutes of the classroom buzzing, a few pairs would grow frustrated, realizing that the task was pushing against their background knowledge's limits. Or, for those who take a Vygotskian "zone of proximal development" perspective, you could say that what was being asked of my students was a bit harder than what they could accomplish without assistance.

Circling the classroom from table to table, I would watch and listen to each pair closely—gathering evidence based on their conversations and behaviors—searching for signals that their frustration might be leaning toward disengagement. When I saw that a threshold had been crossed, I slyly approached a pair of students and melodramatically snuck the first of a series of clues onto their table. Feigning spy-like movements, I would slowly slink away, wink over my shoulder, and watch as each pair peered at their clue, using it to build upon and enhance their background knowledge. The sum of these teacher moves—in-class and on-the-fly differentiation (via observational evidence) combined with a scaffolding resource (the clues)—encouraged each pair to reengage in the challenge.

After my observations, check-ins (a.k.a. formative assessments), and distribution of clues led me to believe that a critical mass of groups had arrived at their best possible solution, I asked table pairs to split up. In the spirit of exploring multiple pathways to a particular answer, I required each pair to decide which partner would stay at their table and which would set off across the classroom in search of new ideas. The student that stayed behind to teach was called the "explainer," while the one that left their table seeking new evidence from other tables to inform their current understanding of the water supply system was the "gatherer." In this manner, I had combined two popular learning activities—a "gallery walk" and a "jigsaw"—to create a new, yet still recognizable routine.

Typically, a "gallery walk" asks students to visit (in silence or barely audible whispers) a series of stations set up around a classroom room in pursuit of learning new information. In contrast, a "jigsaw" asks each individual in a group to become responsible for expertly learning a piece of information (usually connected to a text) and then sharing their knowledge with their partners. Independently, both activities are great ways to help students build their background knowledge; combined, they can be even more powerful. Drawing upon the station-centered structure of a "gallery walk" and combining it with the "student becoming an expert" frame of a "jigsaw," I sought to help my students both extend their nascent understanding of their water supply system and become co-teachers and co-constructors of each other's knowledge.

Putting my "gallery walk + jigsaw" construct into action, students moved around the room and interacted with their classmates. At each table (or station), the "explainer" would share and detail their rationale for the order in which they sorted their water supply cards to each student "gatherer," after which the newly combined partners would offer suggestions to one another. While students chatted, I carefully listened. This practice of teacher-as-observer is an often overlooked but nonetheless powerful pedagogical move that can help educators identify misconceptions and adjust their instruction both in the moment and for future learning. Listening to student conversations in my classroom, I overheard promising ideas inferences such as, "Perhaps that aqueduct card might be better placed after the treatment facility, and that watershed image may be more appropriately positioned closer to a reservoir card." Each snippet of conversation provided information that I could use to instruct and inform, preparing me for when students returned to their original tables.

Upon returning to their initial pairing, students would be given one last opportunity to finalize their perceived understanding of their water supply system. Finally, I would ask each group to "lock in" their answers by sketching and labeling the arrangement of cards on their table. Students would want to know if they "got it right"; however, instead of revealing the answer (watershed—reservoir/dam—aqueducts—treatment facility—city pipes—home pipes—faucet), I would ask students to focus on their process. Pretending not to hear the classroom's cries that I reveal the correct order, I would share with my students that I was proud of how they had engaged in the lesson, hinting that the learning journey itself was more important than their water supply's final destination. By emphasizing process over product to my students, I was attempting to demonstrate how a community of learners has the capacity and power to solve a common problem. And while my delay in the big reveal was typically met with playful groans and continued requests, I would share that the order of their water supply's route would not be revealed by me that day, but rather by each of them somewhere downstream.

Interdisciplinary Ideations / Science + History / The Drinking Water Infrastructure of NYC

For my students to truly appreciate the engineering marvel of New York City's water supply, it was essential for them to learn about its history. Indeed, I always felt that weaving history into the units I taught made for compelling storytelling and provided contextualization for why and how certain things we were learning about came to be, while also giving a nod to the oft-referenced giants' shoulders from which many scientific discoveries and technological advancements spring forth.

To begin our historical dive into the water supply, we constructed a timeline of the significant events that led to New York City's realization that it needed to seek a fresh supply outside its geographical borders. As students sorted the various historical events across their tables, they learned that Manhattan—or Manahatta (hilly island), as it is known to the Lenape people—lacked enough fresh water to support a growing colonial population. The city initially gave the task of solving the water shortage problem to private industry; however, Aaron Burr's Manhattan Company, which would later become Chase Manhattan Bank, failed to provide a clean source of drinking water to city residents.

As solutions to the water crisis—both those conceived by private industry and the city's leadership—continued to flounder, the little fresh water available in Manhattan was continually polluted by the raw sewage New Yorkers haplessly threw upon the city's streets. During the nineteenth century, these unhygienic conditions led to one cholera outbreak after another. Things eventually became so bad that city residents, including children, took to drinking beer to avoid imbibing water from the local well and, to make matters worse, a large fire in 1835 destroyed large swaths of the city (fire hydrants did not yet exist), which finally convinced city planners that a steady stream of fresh water was needed.

With the waters of the Hudson being too salty and the volume of the Bronx River inadequate, city officials needed to look further afield to solve the water crisis. Turning their attention forty or so miles north, they deemed the Croton River, in what is now Westchester County, sufficiently clean and plentiful in volume. Soon construction to impound the Croton's water and bring it to the city started in earnest. This "East of Hudson" water soon snaked underground through brick-and-mortar tunnels until it reached the Bronx. On the matter of the route from the Bronx, a decision needed to be made: dig a tunnel under the Harlem River (less expensive and invisible), or construct a bridge (more costly, but an ostentatious declaration to the world that New York as a city had arrived)?

Being New Yorkers themselves, my students were not surprised to learn that the "build the flashy bridge" option ultimately won out. This decision resulted in constructing the oldest standing bridge in New York City. Completed in 1848 and named the Highbridge, this Roman arch–inspired aqueduct was instrumental in bringing a fresh and steady supply of water to city residents—it literally washed away the filth accumulating in the city's streets. Today, the Highbridge no longer carries the city's water; after sitting dormant for over forty years, it now serves as a pedestrian footbridge (re)connecting the Bronx to Manhattan. The Highbridge span also happened to be only a few blocks away from my school, and every year, I would take advantage of the retired aqueduct's proximity to connect my students to the history of New York City's water supply.

Partnering with Experts: Localizing Learning

To teach my students about the Highbridge, I tapped into NYC H_2O—a nonprofit dedicated to educating the public about the water ecology and supply of New York City. My partnership with NYC H_2O began soon after an educator at the Bronx River Alliance shared with me the contact information of math teacher-turned-NYC H_2O founder Matt Malina.

Seeking to craft new curriculum centered on our city's water supply, I emailed Matt, a bespectacled native New Yorker with a close-cropped dusting of hair and a gregarious disposition, in search of water-related ideas and resources. Upon his reply (and in addition to the water-related suggestions he provided), I was invited on a bike tour of the Old Brooklyn Waterworks—which can, in some ways, be thought of as the borough's equivalent to Manhattan's old Croton water supply detailed above. Cruising around Brooklyn with Matt and a small cohort of NYC water supply history and biking enthusiasts not only fed into my passion for getting outside and exploring my local environs but also opened my eyes to the potential that the Highbridge, Washington Heights's very own piece of water history infrastructure, could have in engaging my students in what we were learning in the classroom. Soon after the tour, Matt connected me with one of his water infrastructure expert tour guides, and just like that, NYC H_2O was partnering with my classroom to bring my students to a local piece of their city's water supply history for the next decade.

Of all the things I did as a teacher to engage and excite my students, I felt nothing was more potent than inviting partner organizations and experts into the classroom. Having classroom visitors helped break up the predictability and sometimes monotonous repetition of regularly scheduled class periods for students and teacher alike. Inviting experts into the classroom also demonstrated to students that what they were learning mattered—many of the professionals visiting them had dedicated their education and careers to the work they shared with my students. In this way, classroom partners, in combination with a carefully crafted curriculum, created an incredible synergy capable of amplifying the magnitude of learning for students.

NYC H_2O's educators would typically visit my class the day after students learned about the history of their water supply; we met on the street outside our school. After introductions and proper framing, we trekked south along Amsterdam Avenue, a main thoroughfare in upper Manhattan, toward the Highbridge. Crossing below 181st Street, we circled to a nondescript brick building with a weathered, colonial era–inspired copper emblem of the City of New York hung above its gates. Students learned from NYC H_2O educators that this building brought drinking water from the Bronx (and further afield) across the Harlem River and pumped it throughout the elevated Washington Heights neighborhood. Students would also learn that when this pumping station came online, the aqueducts in the Highbridge were rendered obsolete and subsequently turned off, which was the first event leading to the eventual shutdown of the entire bridge.

Turning away from the pumping station, we continued our walk, crossing over the highly trafficked and noxious I-95 Trans-Manhattan Expressway just before reaching the Highbridge recreation center. Making our way up a gently sloped and winding paved trail, we would find ourselves perched atop steeply sloped Highbridge Park, with the borough of the Bronx in easy view across the steep chasm carved years before by the now sunken Harlem River. Behind us, enclosed by a tall wrought iron fence and brick walls, was the neighborhood pool made famous by the Lin Manuel-Miranda movie *In the Heights*. To our left, like a sentinel watching over the neighborhood, was a 200-foot-tall octagonal tower. Down a series of steep steps awaited the Highbridge itself.

Using historical photographs and stories as aids, the NYC H_2O educators showed the students that the pool behind them, the same one they swam in during the summer, was once a drinking water reservoir, providing the neighborhood and city a fresh water supply. Students also learn that the sentinel tower, known colloquially as the "princess tower" owing to its resemblance to Rapunzel's fairy-tale prison, once provided enough water pressure for the elevated neighborhood of Washington Heights.

As students listened, viewed, and learned about these landmarks, they connected the Highbridge of the past to the Highbridge of the present, their new knowledge prompting the proverbial "light bulb" moment that happens when someone learns something new about something seemingly once so familiar. In these moments, it was exciting to witness my students connecting what we were learning in the classroom to their lived experience and further signaled to me the importance of combining science, history, and the local environment.

A trip to the Highbridge was not complete without actually stepping upon its walkway, and although the time we spent atop the bridge was brief (we had to fit the entire trip into a single class period), the venture was worth it. Standing on the Highbridge's historically reconstructed walkway, students could experience an uninterrupted 360-degree vista of the river below, the roadways around us, and two boroughs (Manhattan and the Bronx). Turning our backs to the Manhattan side of the bridge with the Highbridge water tower looming large behind us, we snapped a class photo (which I would later proudly hang on our classroom wall) and then quickly turn back toward school. Encouraging students to hustle, we labored up the one hundred or so stairs from the bridge's landing to the reservoir pool above and shuffled along the handful of blocks back to school. Arriving out of breath and just in time for the next class period, students reentered the school building knowing that they had, if only slightly, just participated in becoming a part of New York City's water supply history.

Leaving the Classroom (and City) Behind

My students' most significant concern about drinking the water from their kitchen sink was that they considered it "nasty and gross." In teenage-speak, this meant they did not think it was safe. Through years of teaching and conversation with my students, I came to understand that one reason they held this view was due to their cultural and family backgrounds. Most students I taught were immigrants or first-generation Americans from Latin American and Caribbean nations. Many had firsthand experiences dealing with water sources of questionable purity. Students also shared that their views on drinking water were heavily influenced by their families. Common refrains included, "My mother never lets me drink the tap water in my sink," and "We sometimes drink it, but we always use a filter." In these instances where students shared a bit about their backgrounds, I was careful not to cast judgment, but at the same time, I was not afraid to ask them what might convince them otherwise. "Nothing, Dr. Fox," was the most common answer I heard, but I didn't take this almost instinctive response from my students to heart. Instead, I embraced the mantra that "seeing is believing," and for my students to see and believe, I knew we would need to leave the classroom behind; however, to do so, I first had to find funding.

The most important thing for educators to realize about grant money is that its foundational purpose is to be given away. This tenet was sometimes lost on my colleagues, many sharing that they were too daunted or understandably too busy to apply for grants. While I wholeheartedly agree that in an ideal world, educational grant money wouldn't have to exist—all schools would just be appropriately funded—the reality was that if I wanted my students to do extraordinary things outside the school building, I needed to find the money. So, every year I made a point of sitting down and applying for funding.

One grant I applied for, and always received, was made possible by the Catskill Watershed Corporation (CWC) for a trip to visit our upstate watershed. The CWC was birthed from an agreement established between New York State and the Environmental Protection Agency (EPA) that allowed the city to avoid having to build costly filtration plants to filter its water supply, making New York City one of only five municipalities granted this reprieve in the entire United States. This agreement, which also determined that the CWC would be responsible for helping New York City residents (and students) connect to and gain an appreciation for their upstate water supply through educational programming, was how money became available to my classroom for coach bus transportation and a day of learning on the forested trails of an outdoor education center called the Ashokan Center. This immersive outdoor experience that connected my students to their water supply made the additional grant writing and reporting paperwork worth the effort.

On the morning of the trip, students had to arrive about an hour before school started (no small effort for a teenager) to make the 10 a.m. arrival time at the Ashokan Center. As students climbed aboard, their yawns were welcomed by my ear-to-ear grin. I excitedly checked their names off the trip roster and allowed myself to visualize the day ahead. Having been born in upstate New York, I reveled in the opportunity to reconnect to the forests and small creeks I spent my youth exploring and looked forward to sharing this love with my students. Indeed, as the coach bus departed—students settling into their seats to listen to music, eat breakfast, or catch some shut-eye—it was not difficult for me to briefly close my eyes and envision myself riding my black GT mountain bike into the trails behind my childhood home for a day of adventure and creekside exploration.

Reaching the creek after a chain-rattling descent over a single-track trail of dirt and exposed shale, I would drop my bicycle to the ground, slip off my socks and shoes, and dip my feet into the flesh-numbing water. Following the creek upstream, I would approach an old concrete dam and the small pool of water trapped behind it. Therein, I would wade deeper—looking for frogs and macroinvertebrates (small, freshwater-dependent creatures visible to the naked eye). I would wonder at the diversity of creatures wriggling in each scoop of muck I brought up in my hands from the creek bed to the water's surface. Alas, my reminiscing would always be too short, and as the bus rattled across the George Washington Bridge and we left the bustle of the city behind, I would turn my attention to envisioning the day ahead, pensively smiling at the thought that my students would soon be replicating my own childhood adventures and that I would be lucky enough to be alongside them as witness.

Fieldwork Revisited: Content, Context, and Skills

After an hour or so of travel north from the city on the I-87 interstate, the peaks of the Catskill Mountains took shape on the horizon. Soon after our coach bus exited the thruway, its transmission's audible downshift signaled the beginning of our climb into the foothills. Following a short ascent, we veered away from the state highway and wound our way through narrow roads covered in fall leaves—road conditions perhaps not totally appropriate for a fifty-six-passenger vehicle. Along our winding route to the Ashokan Center, we could see New York City "Posted" signs affixed to trees. They alerted us and others that we were traveling alongside city-owned land despite being dozens of miles away from the five boroughs—a powerful and poignant reminder of the city's influence and the seriousness with which its officials protected the source of its residents' drinking water. When we arrived at the Ashokan Center, our experiential learning destination, a youthful and enthusiastic outdoor educator boarded our coach and detailed our plans for the day.

When I booked our trip, I had intentionally pre-selected instructional activities that best aligned with my environmental science course's curriculum objectives so that the fieldwork my students completed would reinforce and extend their learning. The first session was a water quality assessment in which students would use the same skills they learned at the Bronx River to study the Catskill's freshwater Esopus Creek. For the day's second session, student groups of ten would hike through Cathedral Gorge, a small canyon etched over eons by the winding Esopus. My hope was that the sessions I selected would be joyful learning experiences and allow my students to think differently about the quality of their drinking water supply via quantitative and qualitative research methods.

During the water quality analysis activity, students sampled water and searched the creek bank for macroinvertebrates. While using the reagents and equipment necessary to test for parameters like dissolved oxygen and temperature was not new to my students, digging in the muddy shores of a stream for invertebrates was. As students scooped and sorted through mud (much like I did as a child), a new world of wriggly creatures began to take shape before their eyes. Using spoons and forceps, students shuttled mayflies, damselflies, water striders, scuds, snails, and the occasional crayfish or juvenile trout into various collection containers. They learned that by analyzing the types of macroinvertebrates found in a body of water, they could make a determination of its purity. Whereas leeches and black fly larvae can tolerate polluted water conditions, riffle beetles and, my favorite, caddisfly larvae—with the tubular shelters they carry with them wherever they roam—can only survive in the purest of streams. Using field guides, another great students-as-scientists resource, my classes determined that the macroinvertebrates they collected from the Esopus were the least pollutant tolerant. That observation, in combination with the high dissolved oxygen levels and other favorable water test results, indicated that the water feeding the Esopus—the same water we drink back home in New York City—was pure.

Fieldwork Revisited: A Focus on Joy

After lunch, bellies full, we headed out from the Ashokan Center campus for our hike through Cathedral Gorge. Crossing a covered bridge, we walked single file along the winding Esopus creekbank, steep rock escarpments and cliffs surrounding us on either side. Our guides told stories of how the gorge was formed from erosive forces and how the land had been transformed from forest to farmland back to forest again. They shared that returning the farmland to forest had multiple benefits—or environmentally beneficial impacts often referred to as "ecosystem services." Chief among these services, which ranged from increased animal habitat to creating natural spaces for people to recreate, was the positive impact forested land had on drinking water quality. Indeed, forests and the trees within them are essential in absorbing runoff from storms, preventing agricultural waste and other pollutants from entering the water supply.

While the primary purpose of our fieldwork was for students to learn information they could use to inform their opinions about their drinking water, I also knew that bringing students out of the city and into the natural world had other, more joyful, benefits. As anyone who has done so can attest, spending time in nature can feel, and has been scientifically proven to be, therapeutic.[2] While some of my students would protest the duration and intensity of our walk—mainly when they had to scramble, using hands and feet, up a steeper section of the trail—all would nonetheless feel a sense of accomplishment and wonder at the end of the creek trail when we were greeted with the cascading waters of a forty-foot-high waterfall. During these moments, I would reflect on the joy natural spaces have brought me, as both a young child and an adult, and smile along with my students while they snapped selfies to send to family and friends (though that would have to wait until we were back within cell tower range).

Back on the bus, we said our goodbyes to our guides and headed to our final stop before returning to the city. A few miles up the road, we turned into a parking lot, disembarked, and walked a short distance onto a causeway. As we walked further away from our coach, the vista of the gigantic and awe-inspiring Ashokan Reservoir slowly revealed itself and soon became all-encompassing. The panorama sprawling before us was that of New York City's oldest Catskill reservoir, holding upward of 120 billion gallons of our drinking water. From the weir we stood upon, rocky, tree-lined shores stretched for miles. On the horizon, camelback-shaped peaks outlined a forested bowl, perfectly illustrating the concept of a watershed that we learned about in the classroom.

I was conscious at this moment not to "over-teach," instead letting students make connections to the source of their drinking water. Again, cameras were put to good use, signaling that the magnanimity of this place was not lost on my students. Later, many would share that this reservoir experience, along with being surrounded by nature during the gorge hike, was the highlight of their entire day and the moment during which all of the disparate pieces they had been learning about their water supply fell into place.

Once the photo taking began to wind down, we circled up to discuss the day, cementing the connections between the classroom and the field. Before departing, we gathered for a class photo with the Ashokan Reservoir in the background. When we returned to school, I prominently displayed the picture we took (on the classroom wall near the already hanging Highbridge photo), reminding us of our joyful experiences learning in and from natural spaces and connecting them to history and our lived realities closer to home.

Students as Scientists: Using Scientific Reports

A day or so after our return from the Catskills, a glossy booklet entitled *New York City Drinking Water Supply and Quality Report* is waiting upon our classroom's tables.[3] Its contents displayed the results of thousands of lab tests carried out by city scientists and water quality monitoring robots throughout the entirety of New York's water supply. As students flipped through the slick pages, they saw images of their city's water infrastructure and viewed people doing the jobs associated with maintaining and improving the system. Given their recent exploration of their water supply, some students may have even imagined what it might be like to work for our city's Department of Environmental Protection (DEP), either in the city itself or in the upstate watershed area we had just visited.

Toward the back of the booklet, splayed across a half-dozen or so columns, is a multi-paged table with a long list of parameters and collected data. At first glance, the table is overwhelming, but (as we shall explore more deeply in a later chapter) I always felt it was important for my students to be taught the skills to understand how to read and evaluate data presented in this format. I knew that if they could master—or at the very least, develop—the proficiency to glean information from a complex table, they would also be able to use their acquired skills to interpret similar data sets they might be presented with in the future.

To help students understand what they were looking at in the scientific data table, I first asked them to utilize our now-familiar See, Think, Wonder routine. While it's important to be judicious as an educator and not overuse any particular pedagogical approach, I often found that in instances where a complex text or data table was being introduced, the familiarity of an already known routine provided a welcome structure for my students on how to approach their learning. Indeed, when I tried to do both—introduce a new approach to learning and a piece of complex material simultaneously—I would inevitably spend so much time teaching the approach that the knowledge students might have gained from the material was often lost.

After discussing the data table for a few minutes—with students sharing their observations, thoughts, and questions—I would then provide a series of scaffolds to help make sense of the data within the report. First, I would ask students to look at the titles and headings of the table—helping them get the big picture of the report's contents. Next, we would review the list of parameters, revealing the names of the few dozen naturally occurring substances found in New York City's drinking water supply. After that, I would suggest that students examine each row of the report, to teach them to interpret how many samples were tested and the range and averages of these results. Finally, I would help students determine whether the results that had been reported could be used to determine whether their drinking water was safe. Slowly but surely, students would realize that the water quality report they were viewing, with its hundreds of thousands of data points, was a useful piece of evidence; however, there was one parameter that inevitably caught their attention—the presence of lead in the water.

Interdisciplinary Ideations / Science + History / There's Lead in the Water

When a child ingests lead, the metal acts as a neurotoxin, permanently altering their development and cognitive abilities. While New York City and many older cities' water supplies are virtually lead-free, the service lines used to transport water from the street into homes are oftentimes not. Lead pipes, a legacy of infrastructure projects from times past, continue to threaten the health and safety of too many Americans. To learn more about lead and its appearance in drinking water, I would turn to Flint, Michigan, and Newark, New Jersey, as case studies of how mismanagement and lack of investment could cause irreparable damage.

Politically speaking, infrastructure, unless it's woefully inadequate, does not capture voters' attention, and the consequences of kicking repairs and investments down the road, particularly in Black, Brown, and other marginalized communities, is too often the legislative norm. Indeed, my students, many having experienced similar environmental injustices firsthand, were not surprised to learn that Flint and Newark are composed of many low-income and Black and Brown families.

The story of lead in the US drinking water supply, tragic for those impacted by this preventable misfortune, does have some silver linings. For starters, both Flint and Newark have had success replacing many of their lead service lines, significantly reducing the risk of future lead exposure for their residents. Additionally, my class's study of the data table in the water quality report revealed that New York City's DEP adds the chemical orthophosphate to form a thin film barrier inside service pipes, preventing lead from leaching. Students also learned that simple actions like running their tap water until it feels cold, testing it with a free city-provided lead kit (a favorite and rare extra-credit assignment of mine), or filtering it are other ways to minimize their exposure to lead.

Students as Scientists: Opportunities for Measuring Growth

After visiting their drinking water supply in the Catskill Mountains, interpreting a complex data table of scientific measurements, and going through a case study in which they learned about environmentally unjust incidences of lead, my students had successfully built their background knowledge. To assess all that they had learned, I asked them to work as scientists and write an executive summary that would detail and evaluate the health of New York City's water supply.

Had my students' initial disgust about drinking from the tap changed? Would the background knowledge they had built help them realize their drinking water was safe? We returned to the claim-evidence-reasoning writing framework introduced during our Bronx River estuarine exploration to find out. Having my classes attempt this form of scientific writing for what was now their third time in the school year allowed students to implement feedback from prior attempts and allowed me to assess both their growth and ability to apply the claim-evidence-reasoning approach in a new context.

Providing students with multiple opportunities to demonstrate their understanding was a cornerstone of my teaching. While, in this instance, the task format was familiar, the application of the content they learned had changed. This dissonance—same task format, different content and context—could sometimes cause confusion. However, carefully examining an exemplar work sample (teacher or student generated from previous years) and grading rubric would typically clarify and set a standard for what students were being asked to do.

As students wrote their claims about their drinking water's safety, I would guide them and do my best to be impartial, asking them to use evidence to craft their own responses and not appeal to the feelings of their teacher. Being neutral, however, was not easy, and it should be no surprise to learn that I am an unabashed champion of the New York City water supply. Thankfully, when the writing was done and I sat down to evaluate the claim-evidence-reasoning executive summaries of my student-as-scientists, I frequently learned that virtually all of their responses had glowing evaluations of the water they drank—and that filled my teacher's soul with pride.

In this chapter, I began with a call to action for educators to teach their passion while also acknowledging the fortunate position I was in to teach an elective not tied to a high-stakes exam. And while high-stakes testing will likely continue for the foreseeable future, I am also beginning to sense a turning of the tide. With a more mature and nuanced implementation of standards like the Common Core and the Next Generation Science Standards, accompanied by the rise of new technologies like AI that are already altering the landscape of the labor force, many education departments are beginning to tie graduation requirements to "portraits of a graduate" that focus on skills and competencies attainment in as equal or even greater measure than content mastery.

From my perspective, focusing on skills and competencies provides the perfect opportunity for educators to infuse their passions into the curriculum (as long as we do not also lose sight of the importance of obtaining foundational content knowledge). Certainly, when one pursues their passions, they become experts in the epistemological underpinnings of their interests and gain myriad skills along the way. Indeed, when I deeply explored (and shared) my passion for the content I taught, I found that I was not only better positioned to engage my students but also incredibly fulfilled—something I would argue teachers, as evidenced by recurring reports of turnover, burnout, and demoralization, are decidedly seeking.

Bringing my passions into the classroom fed into a gratifying cycle of joy and meant I could share my love of nature with and alongside my students. It allowed me to connect and partner with expert professionals, like those at NYC H_2O, who could take me on bike rides through Brooklyn, guide my students on local explorations of our water supply history, and inspire deeper dives into New York City's water supply system further afield. It led to jigsaws and galleries, projects, and interdisciplinary possibilities. It created new opportunities to explore and deepen my passion and, perhaps (although not the intended outcome), even persuaded some of my students to adopt my interests as their own. So, while myriad factors, forces, and barriers (both perceived and real) may dissuade educators from infusing their interests into the curriculum, they must not let them, because, as I have detailed in this chapter, the pursuit of passion-driven pedagogy is rife with potential.

CHAPTER 4

Experts in the Classroom

Authenticity, Relevance, and Rigor

My student Manny and I climb a set of stairs and find ourselves on stage at the Tribeca Performing Arts Center in Lower Manhattan. We are there to perform as a part of the New York City Department of Environmental Protection's (DEP's) annual Art & Poetry Contest. In front of us is an auditorium filled with hundreds of audience members including students, teachers, government officials, guests, and parents from across New York City and upstate New York.

On one side of the stage is a lectern with the city and state flags of New York. Opposite these is an American flag standing behind a table covered with the blue and green wave-like symbol of the DEP. Back and to the left of the set of stairs is a gigantic screen with a massive photo of the Ashokan Reservoir projected upon it. In the photo, ice flows can be seen floating on the reservoir's surface, and the snow-covered peaks of the Catskill Mountains loom large across the expanse of water. Manny had purposefully selected this image as the backdrop for our performance to provide the audience with a sense of place and connection to his work.

Cresting the stairs and walking onto the stage, I stop in front of the DEP table while Manny continues to walk toward the center of the performance space. Having taken our places, we nod at each other, and the intro to Chief Keef's "Earned It" drops. The prelude to the song fills the auditorium, creating a sense of anticipation. The audience rises to its feet, and our rap begins.

Manny, who had rewritten the lyrics of "Earned It" to promote drinking water from the tap, spits out, "I got all my NYC tap water on. You can try to flex like you don't want it." His lines flash behind us on the projection screen. Together, we nod to the beat as the audience, awakening to what it is experiencing, begins to clap along. To understand how we arrived on stage, a byproduct of weeks of building background knowledge, interacting with experts, and honing our final project—within a learning environment based on my students' interests and rooted in cultural connections—we must return to the classroom.

Mystery Piece: An Altered Learning Environment

During a typical day in my classroom, students would enter, take their seats, place their materials on their desks, and plop a bottle of Poland Spring or another bottled water brand in front of them. At the end of the period, those who had finished the contents of their plastic containers would dispose of what remained in the trash bin and hurry off to their next class. As soon as the last student was out of the door, I would swoop into action, scooping up the discarded empty plastic bottles and secretly stashing them in an empty fifty-five-gallon aquarium in the back of my room. The next day, the same routine would be repeated, and after a few weeks of collection, I had gathered enough bottles to fill the entire aquarium.

Soon after amassing my new collection of bottles, and in pursuit of building upon my students' knowledge from our last unit on their city's water supply, I would empty the aquarium's contents across the classroom floor. Doing so would turn the physical learning environment of the classroom into a mystery piece that would be waiting for my students upon their arrival. As they entered, so many plastic bottles would be scattered across the classroom floor that students were forced to navigate around and through a sea of plastic. While they shuffled past the discarded waste, a visualization titled "Drowning in Plastic," depicting a steady stream of plastic bottles falling from the sky, was projected at the front of the classroom.[1] Accompanying the animation was a series of infographics illustrating how the sales of single-use plastic water bottles create ever-growing piles of waste every hour of every day. The piles were juxtaposed with increasingly higher world landmarks—*Christ the Redeemer* (the height of 54.9 million bottles, roughly the number of bottles sold every hour), the Eiffel Tower (1.3 billion bottles, the number sold every day), and the island of Manhattan (4 trillion bottles, the number sold every ten years). As the visualization continued to run, the pile of bottles growing steadily higher, more and more students entered the classroom. As students wended their way toward their tables, the audible sound of crinkling and crunching plastic—waste thought to have been gotten rid of weeks ago—could be heard underfoot.

As students took their seats, many openly wondered what was going on. However, there was a surprising number who did not. These uninterested, unbothered, or perhaps secretly suspecting students shuffled through the plastic and followed the same routine they carried out every other day: Enter the classroom. Take a seat. Open book bag. Plop a plastic container of bottled water on the table. Start work. While observing these students, I struggled to hide my grin, knowing they were blissfully unaware that they had stepped perfectly into my mystery-piece learning trap.

For our warm-up activity in that class period, I asked students to consider where the bottles strewn across the floor had come from. Some thought I had bought them, others thought I had collected them from other teachers, but not once did they suspect that the bottles were their own. Revealing my collection antics, students' responses ranged from disgust ("you actually took them out of the waste bin? Gross!") to guilt and shame ("I feel bad I contributed to this waste"). Instead of elevating one reaction over the other, I welcomed all responses and then used my environmental lens to deepen students' thinking. I asked them rhetorically, "How often do we think about where 'away' actually is when we throw something out?" Letting this question marinate, I then painted a picture of where our unit of study would take us over the next few weeks, being sure to include our end-of-unit presentations that would take place in front of guests.

Contextualizing Learning: Sharing the End Goal Early and Often

When teaching a unit of study, I found that mentioning an end-of-unit assessment early and often was an essential strategy for my students' long-term engagement and success. For starters, it helped answer the dreaded student question: "Why are we learning this?" It also provided relevance, authenticity, and rigor to our daily classwork. Additionally, when students were building their background knowledge during the earlier parts of a unit, I could allude to how the content they were learning would help them build a stronger evidence-based foundation for their final projects. In this way, by contextualizing what we were doing in the classroom, I was helping my students to see the bigger picture and scope of what they were learning.

At the same time, I was also attempting to create a classroom culture and sense of urgency that relayed to my students that what we were doing every single class period mattered. And on this first day of our new unit of learning—a day when students were confronted with dozens of plastic water bottles strewn across the floor—I was looking to hook them into learning more about how the single-use containers that were a part of their daily routines were the result of a marketing and advertising campaign that manufactured demand and birthed the explosion of the bottled water industry.

Interdisciplinary Ideations / Science + History / The Bottled Water Industry

Bottled water, which started as a niche product, was consumed at a rate of around 350 million gallons annually in the 1970s. A few decades later, in the 1990s, sales skyrocketed when Pepsi and Coca-Cola entered the market. Noticing a decline in soft drink sales due to an increasingly health-conscious America, multinational corporations (including Nestlé) jumped on the bottled water bandwagon to shore up pending profit losses.[2] At first, skeptical consumers openly questioned the need for bottled water. However, it was not long before the powerful marketing campaigns normalized our bottled water drinking habits. Today, bottled water has become the most consumed packaged beverage in the United States, surpassing the mark of fifteen billion gallons of water sold annually—equivalent to more than twenty-two thousand Olympic-size swimming pools.[3]

What's not often thought about by bottled water drinkers (the underlying intent of the mystery piece detailed above) is where all the empty bottles (including those littered across my classroom floor) go when people are finished using them. And while it might make us feel good knowing that most plastic bottles are recyclable, we shouldn't. The reality is that just because something is recyclable does not mean it will get recycled. In the US, this means that only one-third of all bottled water containers with the potential to be recycled actually are—with the remaining bulk taking up space in landfills or polluting the sea.[4] While innovations in the packaging industry should be applauded for their ability to reduce the amount of plastic needed to make each bottle, it's hard to shake the feeling that bottled water—as a consumable product—is a perfect example of how society often prioritizes convenience over environmental protection and sustainability.

Shifting the Gaze: An Introduction

One outcome I had in mind for my students when designing curriculum was the goal of helping them become critical thinkers who could question the status quo. Critical thinking, one of the four C's comprising the Framework for 21st Century Learning (the other C's being "creativity," "collaboration," and "communication"), is often included as an essential competency in many of the "portrait of a graduate" profiles the framework has helped inspire. In my classroom, I tried to foster critical thinking through an approach to curriculum and lesson design I liked to call "shifting the gaze." At base, shifting the gaze (which will be explored more deeply in a later chapter) means asking students to observe and think about their everyday habits and routines slightly differently. While patterns of behavior are something we all need to navigate the world and get through our daily lives successfully, they may also unintendedly harm ourselves and our environment.

For many of my students, their daily routine was to wake up, get ready for school, leave the apartment, stop at the deli, buy breakfast and a bottle of water (or other beverage in a single-use plastic container), come to school, eat and drink said breakfast at a desk, discard waste, and go to the next period. Day after day, I would see this same pattern of behavior (hence my collection of plastic bottles). And because I viewed my role as an educator to be akin to a coach who guided, not a conductor who directed, I was always thinking about and trying to implement strategies that could empower students and help them make their own informed decisions. That is why I scattered dozens of empty water bottles across the floor of the classroom: I sought to shift my students' gaze from that of daily consumers of single-use plastic bottled beverages, unaware of what happens when their containers are discarded, to that of global citizens and critical thinkers who question what and where "away" is when they drop an empty bottle into a waste bin.

Crafting a curriculum and facilitating learning centered on the bottled water industry allowed my students to examine their behavior patterns, shifting their gaze and their roles from being passive participants to empowered actors. During the lessons that followed our opening mystery piece, I intentionally contrasted the purchase, consumption, and disposal of single-use plastic water bottles to drinking water from the municipal water supply my students had just visited, examined, and deemed safe to drink. The result of this comparison and my students' course of study was that some began questioning their daily consumption patterns. For these students, an opportunity to "shift the gaze" and critically examine their past behavior in light of their newly acquired knowledge about the safety of their city's water supply led to the realization that their single-use plastic bottled water drinking habits were negatively impacting the environment, their health, and their wallets. As a result, a new classroom entrance routine emerged. While much of the pattern remained the same (enter the classroom, take a seat, open book bag, take out materials), now, instead of the crinkling of a plastic container of water, what we heard was the audible clunk of a refillable container of water being set down on their desks.

Partnering with Experts: Preparation

When I wanted to assess what my students had learned, I tried to ensure that there were multiple ways and opportunities for them to demonstrate their understanding. And while the claim-evidence-reasoning writing approach described in earlier chapters might be seen as a more traditional measurement of student learning, regardless of which assessment approach I used, I always attempted to make it as authentic, relevant, and rigorous as possible. The benefit of coupling this "real world" approach toward measuring student learning with the use of a variety of assessment formats was that I was provided a more holistic understanding of what my students knew and were able to do.

Within the context of the drinking water learning unit described above, I gave my students both a content test and a longer-term project that asked them to apply what they had learned. In more concrete terms, this involved students taking a traditional end-of-unit test on the New York City water supply system and the bottled water industry, followed by a more open-ended task in which they created an advertising campaign to promote New York City's drinking water. It was necessary to sequence assessments this way because students needed to possess a baseline level of proficiency in content understanding in order to successfully synthesize and demonstrate their learning in their advertising campaign. In the instances where content test results revealed that they did not, I was allowed to reteach in a way that addressed recently uncovered misconceptions. Sometimes, this meant that an entire class was involved in the reteaching of content during a whole-class test review, for example. In other instances, when it was determined that students needed more intensive assistance, I might arrange a more intimate small-group review. The point was that I wanted to make sure that my students' content knowledge was solid before I asked them to utilize their understanding in a summative work product.

Once I felt students' content knowledge was firmly established and before we began what I called our "Tap vs. Bottled Water" project, students spent a class period going "undercover" as investigative reporters (I found that asking students to imagine themselves as playing a professional role could be helpful when looking to weave authenticity into the classroom). Their task was to analyze the advertising techniques utilized by bottled water companies in the hopes that they could "flip the script" on the "competition." After this initial activity, a friend of mine, Sean Miller, an advertising, marketing, and branding expert, joined us in the classroom.

Partnering with Experts / During: Real-World Exemplars and Tools

Sean Miller and his family lived two floors above my own in the same line of the same rent-stabilized apartment building on the Upper West Side of Manhattan for the five or so years directly preceding the COVID-19 pandemic. Quite frequently, our similarly aged children played together in our homes and in the park across the street from our apartments. As our children interacted—bonding over games of tag and mad dashes through sprinklers—Sean and I often conversed. Through these conversations, I learned of Sean's work, realizing that his expertise would provide my students a window into the professional world he inhabited and bring an element of real-world relevance to my Tap vs. Bottled Water advertising campaign project. Wanting to expose my students to Sean's prowess, I asked him to join me in the classroom, and he graciously agreed. Soon after, the two of us collaborated to bring Sean's experience and expertise in the advertising world and what we discussed in our conversations on the playground to my students in the classroom.

On the day of Sean's visit, he insightfully broke down for my classes the components of an advertisement that he worked on for the Humane Society of the United States. The ad aimed to prevent soon-to-be dog owners from purchasing their next canine from a puppy mill—the term for dog breeding operations that prioritize puppy production over humane care. Before playing the ad, Sean previewed the harsh conditions that caged dogs face in puppy mills. He described the challenges that organizations like the Humane Society face in trying to raise awareness about the unjust treatment of animals. To emphasize this challenge, Sean played an archival interview clip of Sarah McLachlan criticizing the practice of overplaying her song "Angel" (the one that makes me almost instinctively see sad puppy eyes staring back at me from the depths of a small cage), stressing how many of us had become desensitized to the plight of animals in need.

To Sean and his campaign team, it was clear that new ideas were needed to refresh and recapture the attention of an audience that had begun to tune out the Humane Society's message. For Sean, this meant focusing on potential dog owners who purchased their furry friends online—perhaps unknowingly—from puppy mill breeders. A selling point often touted by these canine retailers was the speed and convenience with which a new puppy could be purchased and delivered—often as soon as the next day. For the average consumer, the near-instant gratification of next-day delivery of a trendy French bulldog or other pure breed was hard to resist, so Sean and his team tried to one-up the competition.

When Sean clicked play on his laptop, projecting the ad he helped design onto the screen at the front of the classroom, students watched two siblings lobbying their parents for a puppy. The parents, quickly won over, looked at each other and sheepishly smiled. In the next frame, we see Dad click a button on his tablet that puts their "Same Day Pups" purchase into motion. Instantly, we see the puppy they ordered strapped to a harness, which is connected to a drone that proceeds to take flight. The commercial cuts back and forth between the puppy (and several other airborne pups) being whisked through the sky as the family digitally tracks and then physically receives their new canine in their front yard, their neighbors looking on in admiration. At the end of the commercial, the website URL samedaypups. com appears, but there is a catch unbeknownst to the audience. When would-be puppy purchasers type the URL into their browsers, instead of being taken to a shop for puppies, they are greeted with a web page designed to educate them about the harm of puppy mills.

After the clip ended, Sean shared that this relatively low-budget commercial went on to intercept over twenty thousand would-be puppy mill purchases. My students were impressed and completely captivated by Sean's behind-the-scenes look at how ideas for advertisements and marketing campaigns are born. Witnessing the reaction of my students to presentations by experts like Sean, who are masters at their craft, was one of my favorite things to do in the classroom. They had an immense power and ability to fully immerse and engage my students in the work I was asking them to do. Expert visits exposed students to possible career paths, added authenticity and relevance to what they were learning, and helped create a reference point for what professional craftsmanship looks like. All these benefits made the time and logistical organization of setting up an expert visit well worth the effort, pushing the rigor of my classroom teaching and the quality of student work products to new heights.

In the second part of Sean's visit, we walked students through a marketing industry tool called the "creative brief" that we tailor-made specifically for use in the classroom. The brief prompted students with a challenge and then asked them to think through a series of ever-narrower questions to help them crystallize their ideas for their work. For our project, students had to figure out how to encourage more New Yorkers to kick their marketing-fueled bottled water drinking habits and fill up their cups from the tap, with the brief declaring that it was "up to us to level the playing field."

After guiding students through this authentic and real-world classroom application of a creative brief, Sean and I let them work, circulating the room, offering tips and words of encouragement. By the end of class, students had thought critically about their target audience, brainstormed slogans, and begun to compile persuasive, evidence-based content that they would use to convince more New Yorkers to drink from the tap.

When class ended, students thanked Sean for his visit, and he shared that he would see them again on presentation day, where they would share their final products with him and other assembled experts. This departing message, something I intentionally asked Sean to make before his departure, helped to heighten the expectations for student work and the seriousness with which I hoped they would approach the subsequent class periods as they completed their Tap vs. Bottled Water project.

A Word on Group Projects and Student Choice

Providing choices for students and various ways to demonstrate their understanding was a cornerstone of my teaching practice. During projects like the Tap vs. Bottled Water advertising campaign, the first choice students had to make was whether they wanted to work individually or as a group. While one downside to providing students with the option to work in groups was that it became difficult to assess students individually, I still liked to use group projects in my classroom. For starters, working in groups could help develop students' character traits like working well in a team and being able to compromise. Also, most of them leaped at the opportunity to work with their peers because they thought it was a lot of fun. Taking these measures—instilling a sense of teamwork in students and sparking joy in the classroom—is in many ways just as (if not more) important than assessing every single student's mastery to the nth degree.

For my classroom's projects, student groups could be as small as a pair but sometimes ballooned to be as large as five members. Trying to balance expectations between groups of varying sizes, I would adjust the criteria required to satisfactorily complete a project for students who chose to work individually or in smaller groups. This meant that for the Tap vs. Bottled Water project, students in larger groups had to complete a greater number of project components on how to promote New York City tap water (e.g., film a commercial, craft a poster, write a rap song, perform a poem or skit, make memes, record a movie trailer, or propose their own project ideas) than those working alone or in smaller groups. This approach to incorporating student choice into group work (which could be further differentiated for struggling or advanced learners) was by no means a perfect solution, but it did go a long way in making classroom projects more equitable.

Using Expert Visits to Overcome Perceived Environmental Indifference

It pains me to relay how often students in my class shared that the efforts they felt they placed into learning about and raising awareness on environmental issues were pointless or wouldn't change anything.

I found this mindset to be particularly distressing given that virtually all the students I taught were marginalized youth. Oftentimes, it felt like my students had come to accept that the world's (and their own neighborhood's) conditions could not be changed. I would argue that these feelings, a mixture of apathy, disdain, and hopelessness, stemmed from them internalizing the signals from a society whose actions indicated that those in power did not care about the ongoing climate emergency and other environmental and quality-of-life issues in their neighborhood, particularly as it concerned those who were the most directly impacted and in need of assistance (a category that many of my students fell into). As an educator privy to these frequent reactions from students when they are asked to take environmental action, I felt a great responsibility to change the narrative my students were internalizing and knew that providing them with the opportunity to share their work in front of an outside audience was one way to live up to these expectations.

Thankfully, the experts I assembled from my network—consisting of professional and personal contacts as well as former students and alumni of my school—did not disappoint. In particular, this latter group was my favorite of all visitors, because there's just something special about seeing your former students, who not long ago presented their own projects in front of their own panel of experts, return to provide feedback for a younger cohort. Regardless of who happened to be sitting in the audience to celebrate my students, however, the intent of my message was clear—the work you are doing matters and you, despite what the world may signal, have the power to improve the environment.

The message to my students that their voices mattered—one I underscored often—was solidified on the day they presented their advertising campaigns in front of an audience of experts. Indeed, after weeks of intentional and iterative planning (via the creative brief) and drafting and rehearsing rough and final projects, presentation day had arrived. This day, often called a "celebration of learning" in expeditionary learning circles, was an opportunity for students to share what they had created with an outside audience in a format more authentic and meaningful than sharing their work with their peers or teachers alone.

In the weeks before presentation day, as students worked on their projects in the classroom, I found that reminding them that they would share their finished products in front of an outside audience increased their engagement and the quality of the final drafts. In addition, having a "hard" presentation deadline that professionals had rearranged their busy schedules to attend was a strategy that held students accountable, helped them manage their time, and did wonders to alleviate last-minute extension requests (outside of extenuating circumstances, of course). More importantly, though, having experts like Sean in the classroom's front row signaled to my students that the projects they had worked on over the past few weeks mattered. And, if we as educators (and a society) want to truly empower our young people to feel like they can be important players in our civic discourse, we must provide them with authentic opportunities to practice and hone their skills in (as well as outside of) the classroom.

Partnering with Experts: Overcoming Perceived Environmental Indifference

After everyone in attendance, experts and students alike, had settled into their seats, I would welcome and introduce our guests and the celebration of learning would begin. During presentations, each group (or individual), nervous but confident thanks to our pre-presentation rehearsals, would come to the front of the classroom and share what they had created. Each advertising campaign, composed of the various multimedia project components chosen by each group, was an amalgam of hand-drawn posters, children's books, animations, informative websites, and rap songs. Unifying each campaign was a slogan (a component of the creative brief's planning tool and project rubric) designed to promote drinking from the tap and to capture the audience's imagination. It often was a riff on the source of NYC's water supply ("From the mountains to the fountains," or "Catskill fresh"). Or it drew inspiration from more mainstream advertising campaigns like those from Nike ("Tap water. Just drink it") or for dairy products

("Got tap?"). Regardless of how students chose to craft their slogans and kick off their presentations, each was a great way for the audience to tap into the essence of the campaign.

After slogans were shared, groups presented each piece of their project and, when finished, received both applause and critical feedback from the expert panel. This pattern was then repeated over two or three consecutive class periods until all presentations had been shared (yes, a long time to take away from classroom instruction, but I found it worthwhile and was able to compress the time for presentations, if necessary). As a result, students had the opportunity to present in front of a real-world audience of experts in a supportive and celebratory atmosphere and receive unique, rubric-based feedback.

Once our celebration of learning had come and gone, I asked students to take Sean and his colleagues' expert feedback and use it to complete a round of final revisions. This teaching strategy of providing time for revisions after a "final presentation," a practice within EL Education circles that might be called "encouraging craftsmanship" (a concept in the real world akin to professionalism), allowed students to take the feedback they had received and improve their projects. This practice, in addition to students now having had the opportunity to view the work of other groups, was often enough to provide the inspirational impetus to bring the quality of projects up to an even higher level before the final submission deadline.

Celebration of Learning: A Return to the Stage

With the visiting expert feedback implemented and revised final projects turned in, I asked students to extend our celebration by submitting their work into a citywide art and poetry competition hosted by New York City's DEP. The competition, open to any student who attended school in the city or lived within the upstate watershed that was the source of New York City's water supply, sought to connect these disparate communities, celebrate students' work, and promote drinking from the tap. Given the work we had just completed, I encouraged my students to enter.

Entrance into the competition was straightforward, and all students who competed were recognized as "water ambassadors," with each year's best submissions deemed "water champions." The designation of "water champion," an honor bestowed upon at least one of my students each year my classes entered, also happened to be the reason why I found myself climbing the stairs of the Tribeca Performing Arts Center with Manny.

The beat drops, and my rap partner, who has dubbed himself Manny *Tap*verez, begins performing. My role is to back him up, repeating the last word or two of each line (known in the rap world as a "bar") and, every so often, trying to insert a witty remark between the lyrics. And while I did my best to come through for Manny, I must admit, being on stage in front of a standing audience of hundreds of people to perform a rap song was a bit outside my comfort zone. Exacerbating my nervousness was the fact that Manny and I had not had any time to rehearse together. Unfortunately, Manny's original partner and co-rapper could not attend the day's celebration.

Feeling hesitant about performing alone, Manny thought about declining the invitation to present his work on stage. Of course, there was no way I could let this happen. Getting Manny (or any of my students) to be acknowledged and recognized by a public audience was just too important. So, there I was on stage, doing my best not to mess up my lines, all while watching Manny—now an expert himself on New York City's water supply—absolutely crush it, demonstrating for all in attendance the power of what can happen when experts are invited into the classroom in pursuit of authenticity, relevance, and rigor.

CHAPTER 5

Exploring City Sewers

Adding Science Labs and Systems Thinking to the Methodological Mix

At this point in the book, I have reviewed several pedagogical approaches that I found helped raise classroom engagement and craft a learning environment connected to the real world and lived experience of my students. In this chapter, I once again revisit these bread-and-butter practices in the hope that sharing them multiple times and in a variety of contexts facilitates their adoption by educators. At the same time, I also explore new actions and approaches centered on integrating a traditional science lab into a systems thinking–focused curricular unit. As you read this chapter, please remember that the unit's details are presented in an idealized form and were cobbled together over multiple school years. Indeed, creating a meaningful curriculum and impactful learning environment rarely (if ever) comes together all at once. Instead, it takes place over multiple years (or even decades). It requires the masterful mixing of previously used learning routines and classroom practices from former units of study that students are already familiar with, with those that have yet to be seen. In fact, it is this blending and layering of past practices with ongoing leaps of faith that makes teaching both a science informed by anecdotal and empirical data and an art form inspired by the creativity and vision of an educator's mind.

A Multiday Mystery Piece

In previous chapters I have demonstrated how I approached incorporating a "hook" or "mystery piece" into a single day's lesson. However, it is also possible, as the example below will detail, to build up a "mystery piece" approach over multiple days. In my teaching practice I found that the benefit of doing so facilitated meaningful connections between the lessons in the opening days of a new unit and provided opportunities to incorporate localized fieldwork, expert visits, hands-on activities, and a variety of other highly engaging interrelated learning experiences for students.

Day 1

My students are standing in a circle near the sidewalk outside our school. Our visiting urban explorer, Steve Duncan, is crouched next to a sewer cover. Steve, wiry with a shock of blond hair extruding from his black baseball cap, is dressed in jeans and black boots. Resting on his shoulders is an orange safety vest with reflective yellow and gray stripes that cross at his chest. A carabiner dangles from his belt loop, holding an assortment of flashlights and a pair of fingerless black gloves. Steve's entire look, a series of intentionally utilitarian fashion choices, allows him to "hide in plain sight," as what we are about to do is definitely not approved by the NYC Department of Environmental Protection.

Steve unclips his gloves from the carabiner and slides them onto his hands. He then picks up a long and heavy rod-like piece of angular metal. The manhole tool he's holding sharply curves at one end into a triangular-shaped handle. On the other, it hooks and narrows into a sharpened point. Firmly gripping the tool, Steve nonchalantly asks, "Who wants to see what it looks like inside a sewer?" My students creep closer as Steve takes the pointed end of the metal rod and inserts it into one of the small openings on top of the sewer cover. Firmly gripping the triangular end of the tool, Steve bends his knees and slides the sewer cover off its moorings with a deft and forceful tug, emitting a loud scraping sound of heavy metal on asphalt. To my relief, no heads turn our way.

Wisps of steam and a slight, but surprisingly not too noxious, smell greets our olfactory glands. Students crowd around and peer down into the exposed sewer system, a piece of infrastructure that rarely sees the light of day or captures the public's attention unless something has gone terribly wrong. Steve unclips the flashlights from his belt loop and passes them to students. They quickly flip them on and direct their light beams into the abyss. The illuminated depths below street level reveal the iron rungs of a ladder built into a decades-old column of brick and mortar. Below the ladder's last rung, light reflects off a softly flowing current of gray water. Steve explains, "What we are seeing is a combination of the wastewater that flows down the drains of your school building and the water that was collected underground from the streets during the last rainstorm." This commingling of wastewater and stormwater is a hallmark of older cities like New York, and together, they create a combined sewer system.

While students take turns peering into the sewer, others ask Steve questions about where the water is going and what will happen to it when it arrives at its destination. Their questions are perfect mystery-piece ponderings to open our next unit on the operation of our city's sewer system and the health of its harbor.

Day 2

After piquing my students' interest during the previous day's mystery piece, it seemed only natural to expand their initial sense of curiosity by taking a closer look at a sewer's contents. That is why a five-gallon jug filled with greenish-blue water and various floatables rests on a table next to the doorway of my classroom. This positioning of the jug is critical, as its proximity grabs my students' attention as they enter and allows for the detection of a nose-tingling odor for those daring enough to venture close.

Inside the jug, labeled "sewer water," is a random assortment of materials that I collected from the classroom—eraser shavings, pen caps, dried chewing gum, a few cups of dirt, cotton balls, ripped pieces of paper, blue food coloring, and a healthy dose of vinegar. "That's nasty," and "Eww, what is that!?" are the most common refrains I hear from students as they walk past. "Oh, don't worry, that's just some sewer water from yesterday," I deadpan.

On each student's table, there is a bin of materials. Inside the bins are various pieces of equipment and chemicals needed to replicate the steps of the wastewater treatment process. Alongside each container is a detailed procedure that, if followed correctly, will transform the "sewer water" into something resembling the water from one's tap. Being conscious of the ever-ticking clock and the never-enough-time feeling of a science lab day, I announce, "Whichever group can get their water the cleanest is today's champion," before stepping back and letting students get to work.

While it can often be helpful to let students review a lab procedure before starting a lab activity, in this instance, I felt the straightforward nature of what students were being asked to do made this practice unnecessary. In addition, framing the activity as a competitive challenge, coupled with the fact that students were trying to follow a procedure for the first time, added another layer of the unknown to this mystery piece.

As students got to work, they acted like water quality scientists—aerating, coagulating, flocculating, settling, and filtering their "sewer water." And while this lab activity could be critiqued as "cookie cutter" for its recipe-like procedure, I nonetheless found that it was a great way to give students a sense of what was possible when science and technology combined to purify unsanitary water. Students who were able to successfully interpret and carry out the steps of the procedure slowly but surely began to see the water from the "sewer" change.

First, the aeration process released some of the noxious smell. Next, coagulation and flocculation helped remove larger solid materials. Finally, filtration allowed odorless and relatively clean-looking water to be collected. Typically, by this point in the class period, time was not on our side. Inevitably, many students had to rush to complete the procedure. However, if time did run out, I would always allow students to come back later in the day if they were able to and interested in finishing the entirety of the lab.

Day 3

Upon entering the classroom the next day, students would find a long row of cups haphazardly arranged where the "sewer water" jug had stood the day before. As they passed the row on the way to their seats, many would excitedly look for their own filtered cup of water, trying to determine whether their group's scientific pursuits from the previous day had been the most successful. Standing at the front of the classroom, momentarily delaying the revelation of the science lab competition's "winners," I would ask students to reflect on the activity from the day before, requiring them to detail their responses in their lab notebooks. This debrief opportunity, a practice I found helpful in ensuring that the concepts covered in a lab became clear and concrete for students, often resulted in many remarking that they were surprised to learn that the "sewer water" they viewed from the street on day one of the unit and worked with the day before at their tables could ever return to a clear and odorless form.

Debrief complete, it was time to reveal the "sewer water" champions. To do so, I would utilize our classroom's digital document camera (a modern-day version of an overhead projector) to display each group's treated cup of "sewer water" on the wall. Then, using side-by-side comparisons, cups containing water of lower clarity were eliminated until only two remained. From this final pair, one cup was deemed the most successfully treated and, more excitingly, the "sewer water" champion. Each group's reward? Ephemeral bragging rights. Mine? A class of students primed—thanks to a multiday mystery piece approach—to explore their sewer system more deeply.

Incorporating a Systems Thinking Approach

To leverage the excitement generated in the classroom during the multiday mystery piece, I would next ask my students to explore the terminus of the sewer system and learn how a wastewater treatment plant operates. Understanding how this complex system works—an idiosyncratic blend of science and technology—became all the more relevant for students when I informed them that after mastering how sewage is cleansed, they would tour one of the city's fourteen waste-water treatment plants.

To teach students about complex interdependent processes such as a wastewater treatment plant, the human body, and ecosystems, I would employ a systems thinking approach. I saw systems thinking, a problem-solving and critical thinking skill aligned with the Framework for 21st Century Learning and one of the seven "Crosscutting Concepts" of the Next Generation Science Standards (NGSS), as a way to help students acquire a more holistic understanding of what they were learning and, consequently, appreciate how individual parts became essential components of a synergistic whole. Indeed, the creation and increased implementation of both the Framework for 21st Century Learning and NGSS in schools and classroom curricula has marked a significant shift away from course content being taught as a siloed body of content toward an interdisciplinary understanding and skills-based application representative of what a student knows and is able to do.

I also saw systems thinking, which essentially asks students to become familiar with the "trees" and the "forest," as a means to address a common critique of content-centered science (or any subject matter) education—namely, that material is often taught in a disjointed and disconnected manner. Consequently, without being taught the inter-related nature of a particular subject's body of knowledge and how it is beautifully intertwined (the forest), students may view a course's content as little more than a series of unrelated facts and vocabulary words that must be memorized (the trees).

To address this perceived notion, I utilized a modified "jigsaw activity" (first presented in chapter 3) to teach my students about the inner workings of a wastewater treatment plant. I found this popular activity particularly useful when implementing a systems thinking approach because it expects students to become experts and encourages classmates to teach each other.

To integrate a systems thinking approach with a jigsaw activity, I would create student groupings of four and ask each to master a single step of the wastewater treatment process. The goal for each group was to teach their classmates what happened to the "sewer water" during their assigned step. To do so, student quartets designed and presented their step using teacher-provided resources. In this manner, each "expert group" became responsible for applying their newfound knowledge to teach about one part of the overarching system to their peers.

Asking groups to become experts on one step of a more extensive process and then requiring each to contribute to their class's understanding of a system was a great way to hold students accountable and encourage them to learn more deeply. From an accountability standpoint, it was clear that if a group slacked or could not teach their peers about their step, the entire class's learning would be incomplete. And from a content understanding perspective, asking students to teach each other has been empirically demonstrated to increase their knowledge and connections to the material they have learned.[1]

To formalize and add rigor to a jigsaw activity, I liked to have students share their newly gained expertise during a "presentation day." During presentations, "expert groups" presented at the front of the classroom while the rest of the class did two things. First, students were required to take notes on each step of the wastewater process, incentivized by knowing that whatever they wrote down could be utilized (in this instance) for an upcoming quiz. (I sometimes employed open-note tests when students were introduced to large amounts of new content and vocabulary in a short period of time.) Second, each group was responsible for scoring their classmates' presentations—a strategy that helped students stay engaged and practice the skill of critique. Collecting each group's scoring of the presentations also provided an interesting point of reference when I sat down to grade. And while peer critiques did not make up the entirety of a group's grade, reviewing the feedback students gave to each other often allowed me to pick up on something I may have initially overlooked, such as a commendation noting the use of fantastic images, or an observation about an area in need of improvement, such as the low volume of a group's presentation.

Presentations complete, content quiz given, and a system thinking approach to teaching enacted, it was time to further cement my students' understanding of how a wastewater treatment plant operates. To do so, we would leave the classroom behind once again and extend our learning environment to the city around us. And while touring your local wastewater treatment plant may not be on your bucket list, it is an adventure that I highly recommend. Indeed, viewing the entrails of a treatment plant's pumps, pipes, and pungencies can connect one to water, as my students would soon discover, in unforgettable ways.

Localized Learning: A Trip to the Wastewater Treatment Plant

After taking three different subway lines, including the infamous or, depending on who you ask, beloved Queens-to-Brooklyn G train (the only subway line that does not travel into Manhattan), we cross McGuinness Boulevard and walk along Greenpoint Avenue. A few minutes later, the largest of New York City's fourteen wastewater treatment plants, which collectively services over 1 billion gallons of water daily, comes into view. At the entrance to the treatment plant, we are greeted by the large rectangular bright-orange brick facade of the Visitor Center at Newtown Creek Wastewater Treatment Plant.

Slipping inside the building, we climb stairs that zigzag through the water-themed atrium. While ascending, we peer over the plate glass railing of the staircase onto an undulating ramp that winds through a fountain on the ground floor. The layer-cake design of the fountain, combined with the ramp that winds atop it, reminds us of the dam spillway we traveled past on our visit to the Ashokan Reservoir in upstate New York a few weeks before. Here, the source of our city's drinking water is physically represented at its final destination, and the visual similarity between the two cements the vital link between the water we drink and the water we discard.

Cresting the stairs, we are greeted and escorted by an educator from the New York City Department of Environmental Protection into the Visitor Center's learning classroom. We settle into the blue vinyl chairs, and our tour begins. After a short introduction, which includes reviewing the just recently learned steps of the wastewater treatment process, we leave the confines of the classroom and traverse a long hallway.

Our guide for the day, Jim Pynn, is the plant manager and a veteran of the DEP. Jim's enthusiastic tone conveys that dealing with our city's wastewater is a passion and a source of pride. To begin our tour, he shares a story about how he started working at the plant decades ago in an entry-level position and slowly worked his way up to his current executive role, exposing my students to a real-life example of how hard work and dedication can pay off and how the professional world connects to the science we are learning in our classroom.

The first stop on our tour brings us inside a control room full of dials, switches, and computer monitors. As we enter the room, the plant's engineers warmly greet us, and Jim explains the around-the-clock monitoring necessary to keep a massive plant like Newtown Creek operating. While Jim talks, we look down from the control room onto an enormous room containing the gigantic turbines used to generate enough energy to meet the plant's ceaseless demand before descending a set of stairs and entering the plant's noisy (and quite pungent) screening room floor—or, thanks to our classroom learning, a location known to my students as step one of the wastewater treatment process.

The loud noises on the screening room floor stem from the whir of the energy-generating turbines and a series of hydraulic machines that rake up and then deposit half-dissolved toilet paper and other pieces of trash into large dumpsters, their contents destined for landfills. The smells we detect waft from each container of screened detritus, successfully capturing my students' full attention, as signaled by their audible displeasure and nose-pinching body contortions. And while some students are mesmerized (like me) by the process, others are filled with joy when Jim informs us it's time to move along.

As our tour continues, students catch glimpses of each part of the wastewater treatment process they just taught each other in the classroom. The same series of steps and machinery—settling tanks, primary and secondary treatment, aeration, and so on—now turn into firsthand learning experiences. This reactivation of schema reinforces the systems thinking required to fully understand the structural enormity and overarching function of the plant.

During the last stop of the tour, we ride an industrial elevator that transports us multiple stories upward. The elevator doors open and we step into a glass-domed walkway that links the plant's digester eggs, resembling eight upturned metallic onions, their bulbous shape ideal for the breakdown of the waste removed from sewer water. Standing atop the walkway, we enjoy the uninterrupted views of the sprawling treatment plant below and the inspirational skyline of Manhattan in the distance. As my students snap photos, it is clear that they are enjoying the experience and the vista.

After an extended period of sightseeing, Jim asks us to crowd around a porthole perched atop and directly in the center of one of the digester eggs, whose bulbous top juts into the small circular glass room in which we have gathered. After much shuffling and jostling for a better look, students have packed in tight. Then, with a quick upward motion, Jim "burps" the digester egg by opening the porthole—causing an invisible plume of methane gas to be released into our cramped quarters. Not surprisingly, students react strongly, immediately putting as much distance between themselves and the open porthole while emitting their own noxious sounds and contorting their bodies in disgust. A few moments later, however, groans and contortions turn into laughter, and as Jim recaptures our full attention, students loudly share their reactions to the full sensory experience provided by bacterial anaerobic digestion, the biological process playing out in the digester egg's immediately below our feet that turns waste into natural gas.

As we turn back toward the elevators, our visceral exploration of a wastewater treatment plant has reached a very natural conclusion. However, as the bulk of the group departs, some students continue to linger, snapping a final selfie with their noses plugged, thumbs turned down, and a "stinky" face near the porthole. During these final minutes of our tour, I also take a moment to soak in the city skyline, reflecting on the power that mystery pieces, science labs, systems thinking, connections between curriculum and the local environment, and interactions with experts can have on engaging students and shaping a learning environment. All powerful pedagogical practices that shift teaching away from a hastily covered and siloed curriculum toward a more holistic and deeper understanding of the world.

However, and as noted earlier in this chapter, the confluence of the actions and approaches that helped inspire and inform my environmental science class did not happen overnight. Instead, as with the adoption of any new approach to teaching, it took many years of trial, error, reflection, iteration, and recommitment. It required me to send emails to experts, coordinate trips, set up science labs, and think deeply about the learning environment I wanted to create for myself and, more importantly, my students. Sometimes, experts had last-minute conflicts; frequently, students forgot to turn in permission slips; and every so often, students might use science materials recklessly. Despite the extended time spent planning and in the face of the possibility of chaos, my preparation improved each year. Even with the substantial limitations placed on me by a system that could stifle partnerships, limit opportunities to take students out of the school building, and constrain hands-on activities, I experienced a modicum of success. And while my vision of success was sometimes tainted by compromise necessitated by logistical constraints and bureaucratic oversight, I nonetheless realized success was possible. That is why I encourage other educators looking to craft similarly meaningful learning environments in their classrooms and school buildings not to feel like they need to do everything at once (even though systemic inequities provide much impetus and urgency to do so). Feeling the need to do everything at once can be overwhelming, creating a real risk of contracting "pedagogical paralysis"—a disease that one could argue has cemented our outdated education system in place for far too long. Instead, I recommend (again) that educators start small. Then, after each attempt, reflect, refashion, and retry. Next time, add one more thing. Prove to yourself, your students, and your colleagues that your pedagogy can positively influence educational outcomes. Then, do it again. Crank upon the flywheel, having gained the confidence to go a little bit bigger and be a bit bolder. Before the next turn, who knows? Perhaps the wheel starts spinning along faster than you ever thought possible, generating enough momentum to turn your dreamed-of learning environment into reality.

CHAPTER 6

The Critical Examination of a Harbor's Health

A Deep Dive into Data and the Creation of Community Scientists

Beau Ranheim, the section chief of the NYC's DEP Marine Sciences Division, is hard to miss as he and his colleague Jih Shyu walk down the hall toward my classroom. Beau and Jih are wearing neon-yellow bomber jackets and pushing a flatbed cart stacked with high-tech water monitoring equipment ahead of them. As the scientists and their equipment approach the classroom, students in the hallway cling to the walls, creating a scene reminiscent of the splitting of the Red Sea. At the threshold of my classroom, the two experts deftly maneuver their cart through the doorframe and begin setting up their equipment at the front of the room. Throughout the next class period and subsequent weeks, the data these scientists and their equipment collect for the public good will be analyzed by my students, allowing them to better understand the health of their city's harbor.

The visit by Beau and Jih represents an authentic connection to the environment and a community of scientists. Their presence exposes my students to what practicing scientists look like and do and provides another example of how a learning environment can expand beyond a classroom's walls. In addition, Beau and Jih are a real-world example of how the ability to analyze and interpret data (an essential practice of science and engineering identified by the NGSS) is utilized in the workforce, providing inspiration and a rationale for making data science a central theme of our upcoming unit on the water quality of New York Harbor. Indeed, teaching students how to analyze and interpret data and providing them with extended opportunities to interact with and interpret it is increasingly important. Today, the internet, smartphones, social media, deep fakes, and rapidly changing AI technologies inundate young people with tidal waves of data, necessitating the explicit teaching of skills to help them make sense of it all for their own (and our society's) benefit.

Out of necessity, I invited Beau and Jih into my classroom instead of arranging for the class to visit them. Their regular place of work in open water bays and tight tidal streams makes it impossible to carry out my preferred pedagogical process of having students collect data for their own projects. Thankfully, the two visitors could bring the equipment they employ and the fieldwork methods they complete each day into the classroom. And with their flatbed cart's water samples, electronic sensors, and chemical reagents used to monitor the water in our city's harbor now fully unloaded, my students were poised to experience what it was like to be a DEP scientist.

On a typical day, DEP field scientists like Jih set out into New York's waterways on their research vessel, the *Osprey,* to collect and analyze water from a handful of the seventy or so water-sampling locations scattered across the harbor. The sampling locations can be found in the open water of rivers and bays or distributed throughout smaller tributaries in one of the four sections that comprise greater New York Harbor. The geographic range of waterbodies sampled stretches from the Hudson and East Rivers on either side of Manhattan, to the southern tip of Staten Island and as far east as Jamaica Bay, Queens, where busy JFK International Airport is nestled.

Most of the open water tests done by Jih and the rest of the Marine Sciences team take place aboard the *Osprey,* with some version of NYC's water monitoring program having existed for over one hundred years. And while early monitoring programs were conducted at fewer stations and from the planked seats of rowboats, not the decks of multimillion-dollar research vessels, Beau makes sure to highlight for students the connections between the present day and the past by explaining that the same tests (and their data) conducted over a century ago are still relevant today. This last fact, regarding marine scientists' ability to trace, track, and analyze the changes to the health of the harbor going back decades, is, as my class shall soon learn, crucial not only for understanding whether environmental restoration efforts have been successful but also for making decisions about how to improve the harbor's health into the future.

To underscore Beau's point about the links between the past and present day, Jih and two student assistants test a water sample for dissolved oxygen using the century-plus-old Winkler Method in tandem with modern-day electronic probes. The Winkler Method, still in use on board the *Osprey* today, was first developed and perfected in the late 1800s, and the fact that a century-old diagnostic test is still relevant and utilized in modern times embodies what it means to stand on the shoulders of giants.[1] Indeed, without the development and sharing of discoveries and the dedication by the scientific community to the gradual accumulation of knowledge (and data), our ability to advance as a society and make evidence-informed decisions would be stunted.

To successfully quantify the level of dissolved oxygen (DO) in a sample, Jih follows the series of steps necessary to complete the procedure so quickly that it is clear to the entire class that they have been internalized. With dramatic flair, Jih titrates, observes, then shakes and deftly swirls a series of chemicals (including concentrated sulfuric acid) into a glass bottle containing a water sample. The whole test, which Jih pulls off in about a minute, precisely measures the dissolved oxygen in the glass bottle, as confirmed by my students' subsequent measuring of a similar water sample with the modern-day electronic DO probe. And while the probe's ease of use and accuracy is to be admired, Jih's Winkler Method test is carried out so masterfully that had he been located behind the sleek surface of a glittering bar top and not stationed behind the demonstration table of the classroom, one might have mistaken him for a magician-cum-mixologist at a high-end cocktail lounge. Indeed, the student assistants standing next to Jih and the rest of the class were so transfixed watching the series of chemical reactions turn the water sample from clear to brown to yellow to blue and then back to clear again that when the final determination of DO in the Winkler water sample matched the measurement displayed by the electronic probe, they would erupt in applause, acknowledging and appreciating the scientific mastery they had just witnessed.

Beau and Jih's visit brought a certain magic to my classroom, the kind I wish I could have bottled up and sprinkled on the rest of my lessons throughout the year, especially because the humdrum familiarity of daily interactions between a teacher and their students can sometimes dull the luminescence of learning. That is why inviting experts into the classroom, despite the fear it may have stirred within me about turning the keys to my student's education over to a non-pedagogue, was always worth the risk. Sure, the guest could turn out to be a bust, but that is why I was in the classroom—to redirect, guide, and even push what was being shared with my students toward the most meaningful end. And while visitors who were not a great fit were never invited back to my classroom, those who did well often returned year after year and, in some instances, created previously unimagined educational outcomes (some of which will be detailed later in this book).

For those who may be wondering how I was able to convince so many different experts from such a diverse variety of backgrounds to visit my classroom, I offer one word that captures any collaboration's essence: "synergy." The acknowledgment that the collective impact of working together is more significant than any individual or organization working alone. It is a word that helps inform my motto and shape my worldview. In most instances, the mission statements of the organizations I partnered with and the individuals who volunteered implicitly or explicitly understood that coming into my classroom and working with young people was an impact multiplier. Many even shared that they wished that as students they had had the opportunity to interact with experts and explore professional programs while navigating what they wanted to do and who they wanted to be before entering the real world. As a result, virtually all the programs and professionals my students interacted with willingly provided their time or services pro bono. (That was particularly the case for schools like mine that served a high proportion of low-income students and had Title I status.) However, for educators and schools in different financial positions or who desire to collaborate with organizations where service fees are necessary (and I fully acknowledge that program providers have the right to ask for and should be fairly compensated), the advice I would offer is to ask for a discount (if one is needed), because those willing to work with young people are inherently generous and, perhaps, also know that they can attain synergy by working together.

Interdisciplinary Ideations / Science + History / An Environmental Success Story

Every year, the data collected by Beau, Jih, and their dedicated colleagues is released in a report to the public. Titled the *New York Harbor Water Quality Report*, it allows New Yorkers to get a sense of the health of the waterways around their city and make informed decisions about how they interact with the rivers, streams, and tributaries near their homes.[2] For most New Yorkers, however, a water quality report is unnecessary, as many assume that the water around the city is heavily polluted. While by some measures this is still the case (as we shall soon discover), the truth is that the improvement in the water conditions in New York Harbor, where seals, dolphins, and whales are now frequently sighted, could be considered one of the greatest environmental success stories of the last century.

Throughout the 1960s and early 1970s, after decades upon decades of relentless industrial growth and pollution, Americans began to get serious about protecting and cleaning up the environment. Spurred on by activist authors like Jane Jacobs (*The Death and Life of Great American Cities*, published in 1961) and Rachel Carson (*Silent Spring*, published in 1962), everyday people took to the streets and the halls of Congress to voice their concern about the unmitigated environmental degradation they were witnessing. Lawmakers, hearing the American public's cries for environmental action, responded by celebrating the first Earth Day (1970), establishing the Environmental Protection Agency (1970), and enforcing already passed legislation like the Clean Air Act (enacted in 1963) and Clean Water Act (enacted in 1972) with strong bipartisan support—a reality virtually unimaginable in today's politically polarized climate.[3]

Over the next generation, the Clean Water Act and the regulations it inspired resulted in remarkable improvements in the water quality conditions of the waterways across the country—including those comprising New York Harbor. A big part of the resulting improvements were large investments in constructing new or upgrading preexisting wastewater treatment plants (many were only improved after long-fought legal battles between the community and governmental bureaucratic entities). Before these advancements (and environmental victories), it was not uncommon for raw sewage to be dumped directly into New York Harbor; the waste was so prevalent that waters around the island of Manhattan were well known by those approaching by ship for being able to be smelled before they could be seen. Not surprisingly, this olfactory experience stigmatized and likely continues to negatively influence the imagination of present-day New Yorkers and millions of others living close to the bodies of water surrounding or running through America's major metropolitan areas. Thankfully, what we perceive is not always reality. The truth of the matter is that increasingly rigorous environmental policy, waterway-focused watchdog groups like Riverkeeper and the Newtown Creek Alliance, and public education–minded organizations like the Billion Oyster Project and the River Project Wetlab at Pier 40 have worked synergistically to make New York Harbor cleaner today than it was when monitoring programs first began over one hundred years ago.[4]

With the cleaner waters, life has returned in abundance to the shoreline. This can be seen everywhere, from the Hudson River–infused aquarium tanks of the River Project Wetlab to the replacement of the once ubiquitous piers and shipyards dotting Manhattan, Brooklyn, and Queens with pedestrianized plazas, greenways, and parks that are eagerly sought after and demanded by local residents. Indeed, these residents who flock to the newly reimagined and constructed open space along the shoreline now regularly fish, kayak, and even swim in New York Harbor—an action once deemed as unthinkable by many only a few decades ago. All these recent developments were made possible and are continually improved by the tireless work of Beau, Jih, and countless others dedicated to collecting and using the most up-to-date data to inform both policies and environmental action. As we also know, however, and as my students would soon find out, data can be used to tell vastly different stories—or, at the very least, stories that may not always reveal the whole truth.

Students as Scientists: Using Data in the Classroom

As anyone who has spent time in the classroom can tell you, teaching is hard. And while I like to think that I was successful in the classroom more often than not, I must also admit there were many times when the lesson or unit of learning I designed failed to engage my students. Oftentimes, this occurred when I asked students to work with data.

It's important to call out this reality because it is something I feel so-called "experts" in education are prone to gloss over (and perhaps I am prone to do that as well). No doubt, it is vital for those of us in and outside the classroom seeking the best possible learning outcomes for children to be uplifted and inspired; however, it is similarly important to ground ourselves in the reality that not all pedagogical approaches—as poetically as we like to wax about them—are as engaging for students as we like to think they are. Nonetheless, we as educators mustn't lose sight of our larger purpose and should continue to prepare students for the day when they will apply the content and skills they are learning in the classroom to their everyday lives.

To do so, we must find creative and compassionate ways to relay this message to our students and continue to reflect, reexamine, and incorporate best practices into our pedagogy. That is why when I taught my students how to become data scientists, I had glossy copies of the annually released *Harbor Water Quality Report* waiting for them on their tables when they entered class. This public-facing document, a real-world primary source, is one I would intentionally use to help my students become more comfortable and proficient with analyzing and interpreting data (one of the essential "Scientific Practices" of the NGSS mentioned earlier in this chapter).

I used the report because, as I noted at the beginning of this chapter, the current information age produces more data than our society has time to make sense of effectively. Students, too, are not immune to this information overload, and they are often expected to use data to make decisions yet are rarely taught the skills necessary to do so. At risk is young people's ability to join a scientifically literate citizenry that uses and interprets data daily to come to conclusions and make informed decisions that have the potential to better themselves, their families, and their communities. This problem, which I saw firsthand as being particularly acute for the low-income Black and Brown students I taught, was one I hoped an analysis of the *Harbor Water Quality Report* could begin to help rectify.

The *Harbor Water Quality Report* included myriad charts and figures similar to those that students would one day encounter (or had already encountered) in their everyday lives. I gravitated to this report because I wanted students to be aware and well versed on the data that was publicly available to them by law. But, rather than this data serving merely as a bureaucratic check mark, I thought that critically examining this civically provided information and potentially using it to advocate for environmental improvements was one way my students (and all communities) could better hold government accountable. To begin our initial exploration of the report, I explained all of the above to my students, emphasizing that learning how to interpret reports and data could help them and their families determine which places were safest to fish, recreate, or even swim in New York Harbor. My students, haphazardly flipping through the report on their desks (perhaps overwhelmed by the facts and figures within it), often appeared unconvinced. Despite their skepticism, however, the report would serve as a foundational "anchor" text in the classroom, and I would ask students to return to it frequently in pursuit of helping them become more scientifically literate.

The report comprised a dozen pages interspersed with a cornucopia of New York Harbor–related facts, maps, and photos detailing the DEP monitoring program and ongoing efforts to improve water quality. What I asked students to focus on, however, were the pages that detailed the data indicative of the health and safety of each of the four sections of New York Harbor. Working in small groups, students read the water quality results, keeping an eye out for language detailing the levels of measured parameters like dissolved oxygen, fecal bacteria, and turbidity. Then, having gathered the relevant information, they compared the figures in the report to a standard indicative of the water's health.

For example, in the Inner Harbor section, the monthly average level of fecal coliform bacteria in a given year might have been reported to be 22 cells per 100 milliliters, which, when compared to the fecal coliform standard, indicates that this section of the harbor is acceptable for bathing and recreation. Using this comparison method for each of the various parameters within the report, students were asked to aggregate their findings and evaluate the overall health of the harbor section they were assigned, reporting their findings in a short slideshow to the entire class. When the presentations were finished, students had a more complete picture of the health and safety not only of their harbor section but all major waterways within and surrounding New York. This final "whole-class evaluation," which deemed the health of New York Harbor to be excellent, surprised my students. Capitalizing on this unexpected outcome, I next asked students to dive deeper into the data, adopting a depth-over-breadth approach.

Seeking to impart the lesson that data and the initial conclusions it can lead us to may not always tell the whole story, I asked students to take a second look at the report. I viewed this reevaluation of the data as a chance for students to hone their burgeoning data analysis skills and teach the vital lesson that data—and its interpretation—can often be used to tell a story from a particular perspective. Indeed, depending on how data is analyzed, the stories told can vary greatly depending on the background, point of view, motive, and outside pressures placed upon those interpreting and reporting.

The data we examined in the *Harbor Water Quality Report* was not immune to these pressures. For example, only the averages for each water quality parameter for an individual harbor section were reported. The problem with this approach is twofold. First, each harbor section has monitoring stations that are many miles apart. For instance, the "Inner Harbor" section begins at the Hudson River's furthest point north in the Bronx and stretches thirty miles south to the lower tip of Staten Island. The consequence of reporting an average for this entire range and deeming it representative of one harbor section is that it washes out localized trouble spots that a more granular data analysis approach may otherwise reveal. Similarly, using averages, a rather blunt analytical approach, can hide the existence and possibility of outliers at any water quality monitoring station. These limitations have real-world consequences for understanding the true health of New York Harbor, and they illustrate important data-science concepts that I wanted my students to be aware of and able to understand.

With this critique of the harbor-quality reporting in mind, I asked students to examine the publicly available raw data used to calculate the averages published in the report. To do this, they accessed an annually updated spreadsheet containing every water quality analysis taken for each parameter measured from all sampling stations across New York Harbor. Yes, that's a lot of data. And, not surprisingly, when my students clicked on the link that opened the document containing all this data, collected in hundreds of rows and spread across dozens of columns, they were overwhelmed. Despite this initial reaction, however, I knew that with practice, my students would soon develop the knowledge and skills to use the powerful processing tools of a spreadsheet application to interpret and, more importantly, tell a different story about the health of the harbor than the one published in the water quality report they just finished examining.

Students as Scientists: A Data-Science Approach

When I was a student in high school—way back in the last century— I distinctly remember taking an elective "technology" course in my school's "computer room" that taught me how to use a spreadsheet. The semester-long class (a distant relic of a bygone era) was perhaps one of the most practical I ever completed. Many of the skills I learned therein are those I still use today. I learned not only how to enter and organize data but also how to utilize the various formulas and functions that would allow any given user to fully leverage the power of this digital tool.

Today, learning how to use a spreadsheet software application in a classroom does not seem as commonplace. And while I do not mourn the loss of semester-long classes dedicated to learning the ins and outs of Microsoft Excel, I nonetheless recognized that if my students were not taught how to access and leverage this tool, they would be at a disadvantage when it came to being able to manipulate and analyze data for their own purposes.

Helping students become more comfortable working within a software application required me to teach them how to freeze rows, add columns, and use simple calculation formulas. Thankfully, most of my students, benefiting from being born as digital natives, typically grasped these foundational concepts quickly and, before long, put their newfound skills to work.

Returning to the initially overwhelming spreadsheet of raw data, students would use what they learned to sort results, insert rows, enter formulas, and calculate the averages of each sampling station within their originally assigned harbor section. Before long, students started noticing some troubling findings, "A few of my sampling stations within my harbor section had over twenty-thousand cells of fecal coliform bacteria per one hundred milliliters of water in it," a student might call out. (A value of under 200 cells per 100 milliliters is deemed safe for swimming.) "Mine too," another might reply. In this manner, one group after another would begin to realize that what was reported initially in their glossy booklets may not have revealed the entirety of the story about their harbor's health.

When a critical mass of students recognized that bacteria levels would spike to seemingly unthinkable levels during certain times throughout the year, I would stop and ask, "What do we think is going on here? How is it possible that we just finished evaluating the entire harbor—which we deemed to be in excellent health—and there are all of these individual monitoring stations with bacteria levels off the charts?" While students grappled with and tiptoed around the source of the bacteria problem in our ensuing class discussion, they did not lose sight of the fact that their analysis of the underlying data of the original report had given them new insights about the health of their city's waterways.

Moments like these—something education theorists might refer to as "cognitive dissonance" or, more simply, a point in the learning process where something previously known is challenged—provide opportunities for new knowledge to be incorporated into a preexisting schema, and as an educator, I always tried to take advantage of these teachable moments. That is why, after our class discussion, I would inform students that the secret to understanding the cause of bacteria levels spiking at certain stations was not sophisticated. It merely required understanding how the water surrounding any given sampling station is influenced by localized circumstances. Projecting a map of sampling station locations and then asking students to analyze it allowed them to promptly discern a noticeable pattern. All the instances where elevated levels of bacteria occurred were at stations situated in small tributaries like canals and creeks, not at those found at open water sampling sites located in rivers or bays.

Now, guiding students closer to the underlying cause of bacteria infiltration, I would ask, "What might it be about small creeks and streams that would lead to higher levels of bacteria?" Admittedly, this is a tricky question for students who may have little background knowledge or firsthand experience witnessing the ebb and flow of an estuary. Eventually, however, with the right blend of iterative questioning and slight hints along the way, we as a class would realize that small bodies of water are less likely to flush out anything bad (meaning fecal bacteria) that might accumulate within them.

However, this realization would only lead to additional questions. Namely, "How do fecal bacteria even get into our water in the first place?" and "Isn't all of our wastewater treated before being released into our harbor?" Some students, attempting to balance what they thought to be true (the harbor was in excellent health) with what their most recent data analysis told them, would try to answer. While I would always allow students' curiosity to fill the classroom void, I would also intentionally leave this last question unanswered, fully knowing where our class was headed next—back into the sewers.

Interdisciplinary Ideations / Science + History / The Legacy of a Combined Sewer System

Sometimes, I couldn't help but think that the environmental science course I taught was a history class. Indeed, I would argue that any good course, the sciences included, must tap into the historical context of its content area to allow students to fully understand and appreciate the learning they are engaging in. Without this historical lens, what's taught in the classroom can, paradoxically, feel disconnected from the present day and be at risk of being underappreciated.

This was particularly true when my students learned about New York's water supply and sewer system. Had I not taken the time to acknowledge past public investments of time, money, and people, my students most likely would not have engaged in the learning process as thoroughly. For my students, learning that only a few generations ago, it was not uncommon for people to die in the streets from cholera and dysentery outbreaks caused by fecal coliform contamination of wells and streams went a long way to helping them feel more appreciative of the clean water they now can easily access.

Teaching the history behind the waste and drinking water problems of the past, as well as the decisions made to address them, allowed my students to understand how environmental problem-solving by previous generations may have, yes, solved the most pressing problem of unsafe drinking water but also caused the high levels of bacteria contamination that our reanalysis of harbor data revealed. Indeed, this Band-Aid approach to environmental problem-solving is an essential lesson for students to understand, as I found it helps them further connect what happened in the past to the present day and evaluate how present-day solutions might affect the future.

So how did we get here? How did New York and other older American cities solve their drinking water problems but not fully resolve their wastewater woes? Well, in a race to solve the wastewater pollution problem plaguing drinking wells and streams as quickly as possible, city planners of long ago decided to connect sewer pipes from buildings with the stormwater system that collected precipitation from the street. This engineering approach created a combined sewer system that works perfectly well most days—that is, as long as the weather is dry. However, when it rains, sometimes even just a small amount, some of the fourteen wastewater plants around New York cannot handle the combined sewage and stormwater flow. So, in an attempt (and much-welcomed decision) to prevent raw sewage from flowing back into people's homes and city streets, a mixture of untreated wastewater and stormwater is diverted into New York Harbor, causing a combined sewer overflow (CSO) event.

Unfortunately, CSO events are not uncommon, with upward of 21 billion gallons of untreated water being released into New York City waterways every … single … year.[5] For context, the city's DEP claims that its wastewater plants treat about 1.3 billion gallons of water daily, for a total of 474.4 billion gallons annually.[6] In other words, for about every two dozen gallons of water safely treated, another gallon is diverted directly into the harbor, teeming with fecal bacteria.

When students learn how the legacy of the decision-making behind the creation of their city's sewer system continues to impact their lives, they cycle through feelings of disgust, confusion, and anger. They want to know why the bacterial contamination of their city's waterways is continually allowed (fixing the problem is expensive) and what can be done (lots) to solve it. Thankfully, I also know that students have newfound background knowledge from their own independent data analysis, providing them with unique insights into the problem. The only thing left to do is allow them to take what they have learned and advocate for CSO solutions.

Students as Scientists: Community Science Activists

Over the next few days, the CSO solutions students learn about in class could be placed into one of two buckets. Bucket one was reasonably straightforward—use less water when it rains. This approach to solving the CSO problem asks people to wait a few hours to do their laundry or delay a shower if it's raining. Bucket two is to build infrastructure like green roofs, water retention tanks, and bioswales (sometimes called rain gardens) that slow the volume of water entering the combined sewer system during rainfall.

My students' imaginations were captured by green infrastructure solutions that depend on more natural means and living things that use vegetation to act like a sponge during a storm. Sensing their interest, I asked, "What if every building's roof had a thirsty garden atop it?" and "Why don't we have living walls growing outside our school?" These open-ended questions allow students to envision a city transformed by previously unrealized green spaces, making it more livable and solving the CSO issue. Questions like these also ask students to dream of a cleaner and greener world, awakening their environmental conscience and encouraging them to take action.

In my experience as a teacher, all students agree that protecting the environment in which they live, learn, and play is essential. At the same time, however, these same young people would also share that they felt overwhelmed and even helpless to effect change. One outcome of this reality was that many of my students, before learning about the history of an environmental problem like CSOs and fully grasping the most recent data available, typically defaulted to solving the earth's woes by suggesting we should "recycle more" or "not litter." And while these initial responses should be considered a good start, they also leave much to be desired.

To address the baseline and superficial solutions that students and, if we're honest, most adults default to when solving environmental problems, I would incorporate an environmental activist lens into the classroom. This meant it was not good enough for students only to learn about an environmental issue or policy. Instead, they had to use their recently acquired knowledge and skills (in this case, data analysis) to advocate for change as a community scientist.

Being a community scientist (an individual or group taking part in the scientific process without formal training) in my classroom meant that after my students examined and reinterpreted the data from their harbor, they advocated for action. To do so, the summative assessment of our harbor unit asked my community scientist students to demonstrate their understanding of what they'd learned by creating a public service announcement (PSA) that would educate their audience about the challenges, solutions, and actions one could take to combat CSOs.

Replicating the same project format for students as the now familiar and successfully completed tap water advertising campaign (chapter 4) allowed students to work more efficiently. The students' familiarity with the format also allowed me to spend less time explaining to them how to complete the project and focus more on providing individualized support to each student or group. The product of my additional and more focused attention was more efficiently produced PSAs that were often of higher quality than the students' tap water campaigns created only a few weeks before.

To make their PSAs, students provided evidence from their analyzed data that highlighted the impact of the CSO problem along with suggestions for action. Like the tap water campaigns, each PSA had to have a unique slogan. Many featured rhymes like "Slow the flow, stop CSO," and "CSO's, now you know"; some were even bilingual ("CSOs are no bueno"). These creative slogans were also incorporated across the formats students chose to meet the project requirements, from posters and websites to raps and skits. Like the tap water campaigns, all finished PSAs were presented and critiqued by an expert audience of educators, nonprofit leaders, and academics. The sense of familiarity that accompanied this second go-round of presenting in front of an expert audience as part of a celebration of learning translated into increased student confidence and enjoyment—some even reveled in the opportunity to share their ideas for a healthier harbor with a community of professionals.

At the beginning of this chapter I detailed how inviting experts into the classroom can make magic happen and inspire the creation of an entire unit dedicated to the deep exploration of data. We also reviewed how a curricular path intent on providing students with essential skills to navigate a data-rich world can teach them how to advocate for change as community scientists. Indeed, providing students with opportunities to organize, interpret, analyze, and evaluate data using web-based tools and technologies has become increasingly important, as evidenced by standards like NGSS and the reality of our data-rich world.

Undoubtedly, young people who are prepared to make sense of the data they come across will be better positioned to utilize it for themselves, their families, and their communities, whereas those without these essential skills will likely be left feeling confused, uncertain, and powerless, constituting an entire class of data-illiterate individuals vulnerable to misinformation campaigns and other unforeseen swindles. For this reason, this chapter also serves as a call to action for educators to seek out and create opportunities that help students identify and prevent the pernicious proliferation of half-truths, conspiracy theories, and deep fakes—cultivating the critical lens called for by the data-driven reality of today and tomorrow.

CHAPTER 7

In Pursuit of Environmental Justice

The Power of Professional Partnerships

The environmental injustices facing my students were stark. In northern Manhattan, the traffic and air pollution conditions are some of the worst in the United States—the result of noxious exhaust from diesel-powered trucks that endlessly rattle across the infamous I-95 Trans-Manhattan Expressway and old apartment building boilers fueled by dirty heating oil that belch soot into the surrounding air. Together, the vehicles and boilers create a toxic miasma of particulate matter that can cause and exacerbate chronic asthma—a disease impacting the health of many of my students.[1] To make matters worse, the open and green spaces that could help mitigate the effects of air pollution—not to mention extreme heat in an ever-warming world— were located on the perimeters of the neighborhood and frequently overlooked and underfunded.

The lack of safe, accessible, and well-cared-for green spaces often discouraged students and their families from gathering outside. A dearth of grocery stores and the high density of fast-food chains and bodegas selling cheap food loaded with salt, fat, and sugar aids the rise of already sky-high adult and childhood obesity rates. The confluence of these factors directly increased the chances that my students would face later-in-life health issues like diabetes, cardiovascular disease, and other chronic ailments. This reality serves as a perfect example of what can happen when environmental justice is not carried out—when the right to fair treatment and meaningful involvement in the decisions that affect one's environment and health, exclusive of who they are, where they come from, how they identify, or what they believe, is not protected.

The living conditions of the buildings my students and their families inhabited were yet another example of environmental injustices faced by the primarily working-class Latinx immigrant community of Washington Heights. Compared with the housing in whiter and wealthier parts of the city, my students and their families were more likely to find pests, rodents, mold, and high levels of lead in the walls of their apartments. Exacerbating these housing conditions was the fact that many families lived in multigenerational households, crowding together to make rent in an increasingly unaffordable and gentrifying neighborhood.

All of this is to say that the environmental and health challenges my students faced daily were a poignant reminder of the continual reverberations and negative impacts of racist governmental policies like redlining—the Depression-era federal housing policy that officially designated certain sections of Washington Heights and other Black and Brown communities (or those whose demographics were shifting that way) as "definitely declining" or "hazardous." In my teaching career, I witnessed firsthand how a legacy of injustice shaped my students and their families' lived experiences and infringed upon their ability to pursue their preferred educational and career goals. Too often, my students missed school or passed over extracurricular enrichment opportunities because they needed to take a job for extra income or care for an ailing or younger family member.

As a consequence of my students' lived reality, the classroom conversations I facilitated in hopes of encouraging students to address and take action on environmental injustices often fell upon disillusioned ears. Sadly, the broader societal signals sent to my students that they did not deserve the same safe and healthy living conditions afforded to their whiter and wealthier peers were not only received but internalized.

To push back against these feelings and this mindset that allowed my students to accept the status quo, I partnered with a local non-profit to design a curriculum centered on environmental justice. This new curriculum asked students to critically examine their neighborhood's conditions and become experts on their surroundings. Then, once their background knowledge had been built, my students would use their newfound expertise and, as part of a celebration of learning—in this case, a presentation in front of their community—encourage action for environmental justice.

This approach to curriculum design—that is, one that supports students in becoming experts on issues connected to the local community—encapsulates my belief in how learning environments should be shaped. Indeed, helping students understand (with the aid of partners, whenever possible) how the problems they are learning about impact their lives, and then providing them with authentic opportunities to advocate for the resolution to those problems may, as we shall see below, lead to some of the most powerful learning experiences that a teacher and their students will ever have.

Partnering with Experts: Laying the Foundation

Partnerships were integral to shaping my students' learning environment and experiences in the classroom. Among my varied collaborations, my work with WE ACT, an organization committed to fighting for environmental justice for community members of northern Manhattan, was particularly impactful.

At the time of my initial outreach to WE ACT, I was unaware of how much of a juggernaut it was in the environmental justice (EJ) space. Today, the organization is nationally and internationally recognized for its decades-long efforts to provide voice and agency for the residents of northern Manhattan (and other similar EJ communities), but its success has never come easy.

WE ACT's fight for environmental justice started with an act of civil disobedience. For years, noxious fumes from a wastewater treatment plant on the West Side of Manhattan had been spewing into the Black and Brown neighborhood along nearby Riverside Drive. To draw attention to this injustice, a small group of activists, now known as the "Sewage Seven," chained themselves across the nearby highway, creating an epic traffic jam and catching the attention of local leaders and other like-minded environmental activists. Eventually, after a long legal battle, the Sewage Seven and its newly formed band of EJ advocates forced the city to address the fumes filtering into the nearby neighborhood and build a twenty-eight-acre park atop the treatment plant foundation.

This initial series of victories was followed by several other successful campaigns, including those calling for the elimination of diesel buses from New York City's fleet, the construction of a riverfront park, the creation of a LEED-certified bus depot, and the establishment of a green jobs training program for community residents. My students learned about these stories of success both in the classroom and on an in-person "Toxics and Treasures" guided tour led by a WE ACT staffer—an example of localized learning where students visited sites around the city and heard stories about how WE ACT helped turn sources of pollution into environmentally friendly community gems. The stories of success served an important lesson—that is, they demonstrated to students that people in their community were unwilling to accept the status quo of polluted air and a lack of green space, and that one should not normalize unsafe and unhealthy living conditions just because they happen to live in an underserved community.

My original contact at WE ACT was Ogonnaya Dotson-Newman, an ebullient and energetic woman with a flair for the dramatic. She brought her trademark combination of a carefree West Coast vibe, booming voice, and incredible laugh to each of her classroom visits.

When I first connected with Ogonnaya, I was teaching environmental science for the first time at my new school. Being in a new building, with new colleagues, and teaching a new course to an unfamiliar student cohort was both exciting and daunting. Despite the novelty and uncertainty of my new position, my recently gained understanding of expeditionary learning pedagogical approaches inspired me to make my classroom more engaging, meaningful, and relevant to my students' lives.

One of my first attempts to actualize this culturally responsive approach to teaching (which entails connecting the lived experience of students to the classroom) started soon after Ogonnaya replied to an email I sent her on a whim. In my message, I had asked Ogonnaya if she would visit my classroom and introduce my students to EJ and WE ACT. Little did I know that Ogonnaya's willingness to say "yes" not only would create incredibly impactful, joyful, and profound learning experiences for my students that year but would also set the stage for a beautiful partnership that has continued to this day.

Thankfully, Ogonnaya's first visit was magical, as she instantly connected with my students. Through a dynamic presentation, she shared the work of WE ACT and laid the foundation for our soon-to-be-constructed EJ curriculum and decade-long synergistic partnership. At the time of her visit, however, I was just happy to have Ogonnaya join my classroom, because it meant that I, a white educator teaching a new course in a Black and Brown neighborhood of which I was not yet a part, could collaborate with an expert from an organization that had been fighting for justice with and for the community in which I was teaching—helping me not only develop relationships with my students but also encourage them to recognize that what they were learning in the classroom was directly connected to their lived experiences.

When we debriefed after her visit, Ogonnaya and I both felt empowered by my students' reactions and willingness to engage in environmental justice work. Indeed, many had shared with me that after learning about WE ACT's campaigns, they had a newfound desire to become more aware and involved in what was happening in the community. After I shared this with Ogonnaya, we made plans for her to return.

At the start of the next school year, Ogonnaya shared that WE ACT had written my classroom into a grant to allow us to continue our burgeoning environmental justice work together. This time, however, instead of a few haphazard (yet powerful) classroom visits, Ogonnaya, WE ACT, and other community partners would launch a composting program in my classroom.

Before long, my students were building an outdoor composting system, constructing food scrap–laden worm bins for use in the classroom, and teaching lessons about their work to younger students at our school. This inspired the younger students and their teachers to start their own composting projects in their classrooms. Seemingly overnight, our environmental justice work had become infectious.

It was a beautiful thing. Students in upper grade levels were learning how and why composting food scraps was an environmentally conscious thing to do and using their learning to educate our school's younger students. As the compost program developed, students designed tracking systems to keep tabs on total pounds of food waste diverted from landfills and created a student-run environmental action team whose members stationed themselves in the school's cafeteria to make sure food scraps were properly sorted and carried to the small school garden where our newly student-built composter was located.

Eventually, members of the larger school community took notice of the students' efforts, thanks to an application that a colleague submitted to a contest run by our city's Department of Sanitation (DOS). Like our school community, the DOS was impressed, and the agency granted our school the Golden Shovel Award—a designation given to the best composting program in the city. To this day, it continues to amaze and inspire me that a program that was the recipient of a delightful trophy (consisting of a golden shovel stuck into a heap of compost), along with an award of $10,000 to expand its work, could all be traced back to an email sent to an expert in the local community by a new teacher at a new school teaching a new course.

Partnering with Experts: Building Upon Past Success

As my school's composting program continued, Ogonnaya and I dreamed of new ways for students to address environmental injustice. Our next collaboration looped in another of WE ACT's long-standing partners—Columbia University's Mailman School of Public Health. For this partnership, Ogonnaya and my classroom linked up with a professor who taught a graduate-level course on community-based participatory research (CBPR)—a methodology that asks researchers to work in an equitable partnership with a community in pursuit of positive change.

The idea was for my classroom to be a placement site for Mailman graduate students. In turn, they would teach my students CBPR basics and actively support them in telling their stories through the "Photovoice" approach, which centers and uplifts participants' perspectives and lived experiences so they are more easily seen and heard. In practice, this meant that a few times a week, over multiple months, graduate students and my students worked in small groups as co-investigators to take pictures of the environmental injustices in their neighborhood.

Before long, students had gathered photo evidence of abandoned buildings on their block, overflowing litter baskets on street corners, crumbling staircases, and traffic-clogged expressways. Once the evidence was collected, my students and their graduate school co-investigators used an iterative editing and selection process to choose the images most meaningful to them. To give additional color to each image, students wrote a short caption explaining where and why the photograph was taken and how its subject matter connected to their environment and health.

A final culminating event was held on Columbia University's medical campus to celebrate my students' learning of CBPR and efforts to document environmental injustice. As students presented their photographs in front of their graduate-student collaborators, classmates, and other guests, I watched them proudly share their work and listened to them eloquently tell stories about their hopes for positive change in their community. While this authentic forum and inspiring dialogue made an exciting impression on those in attendance, I also couldn't help but feel something was missing—concrete environmental justice action.

Partnering with Experts: Reaching New Heights

During the next school year, the pursuit of my new goal of teaching my students about environmental justice was bolstered by another

partnership. This time, instead of Ogonnaya and Columbia graduate students, a dynamic duo of WE ACT interns joined me in the
classroom. Together, we adapted WE ACT's adult environmental
health and justice leadership training course for my students. The
curriculum we developed, which after several iterations and years of
use in the classroom would go on to win a statewide environmental
education award, asked students to document the environmental and
health issues facing their community and take action to rectify them.

The curriculum included an introduction to environmental justice followed by five lessons about ongoing WE ACT initiatives, which
covered campaigns focused on toxic household products, open and
green spaces, and climate and food justice—all issues my students and
their families faced living, working, playing, and praying in northern
Manhattan. This initial survey of lessons—intentionally broad—was
designed to help students understand what environmental justice issues were relevant to their lives and help them determine which one
of the five they wanted to explore more deeply.

The lessons were co-designed and co-taught by me and an amalgamation of WE ACT experts. To enhance and add real-world connections to each class, WE ACT's staff joined my students in the
classroom to share their experience and expertise on ongoing EJ
campaigns. In practice, this meant that when students were introduced to the concept of climate justice (the idea that the impacts of
climate change should not fall disproportionately on the shoulders of
those least responsible or prepared to cope with a warming world),
WE ACT's climate justice experts would join us in the classroom. In
this manner, students not only had the opportunity to learn from
experts on each EJ issue but also were exposed to people who had
pursued EJ work as a profession, providing them a window into a
world they too may one day want to explore.

After the opening intro to EJ week, students picked one topic
that was most near and dear to them. Next, groups were formed and
background research began. To speed up the research process, we
provided each group with a curated list of resources related to their
topic, a deliberate move on our part to remove what can be, for many
students, a laborious (and often fruitless) search process. It allowed

groups to focus on quickly deepening their background knowledge from credible sources. And while searching for and finding sources is a valuable skill for students to learn, the expediency of the curated resources and accuracy of the information provided made forgoing this process (in this instance) worthwhile.

In the opening days of research and throughout the project's duration, I would update a student-facing calendar. This daily routine helped put deadlines for research and other project components front of mind for students. It was also essential for helping students structure their time for each class period and provided a sense of urgency for the overarching project.

In addition to pointing out the shorter-term goals and deadlines on our daily calendar, I also reminded students that the work they were completing would culminate in a community-wide Environmental Justice Expo. The EJ Expo, an authentic celebration of learning where students would present work products inspired by their selected topic in a science fair–style event for the public and a panel of judges, was my attempt to build off the previous Photovoice project that saw students successfully document an EJ issue but not fully take action on advocating for its resolution. And while the students' initial reactions to the announcement about the upcoming EJ Expo were often marked by hesitation and even dread, I nonetheless believed in the power of the expo and its public forum format to turn my students into EJ advocates.

In addition to providing an opportunity for students to act on environmental injustice, I found that the EJ Expo also helped elevate the quality of each group's final products, the authentic format signaling to students that the quality and craftsmanship of their work mattered. Indeed, when my students knew that their work would be placed on public display, it not only relayed to them that it was important but also increased the rigor of the task. As these realities combined in the final days before the EJ Expo, students were willing to spend extra hours during lunch or after school revising their work, pushing the quality of their final draft to new heights and paralleling the iterative process that might one day be expected of them as professionals.

However, before we got to our EJ Expo, students often revealed that their hesitancy to complete an environmental action project stemmed from past experiences and similar projects that rarely made it past the classroom walls, along with a general sense that "nothing ever changed." No doubt there were valid reasons for them to have these feelings; however, for me, their Panglossian teacher, I also knew they were well prepared to rise to the challenge, actualize their brilliance, and make a meaningful difference in the world around them.

My optimism stemmed from what I had already witnessed that year in the classroom. Even though students still had to build their background knowledge on their EJ topic of choice, I knew that the other projects we had completed that school year had been preparing them for the EJ Expo and the public forum it offered. The knowledge and skills they had acquired in different learning units—data analysis, close reading, delivering presentations in front of experts—had been intentionally planned with the EJ Expo in mind. So, I knew—even if my students didn't—that they would be ready to embrace their role as environmental justice experts and advocate for change in front of and for their community.

As students wrapped up their research, they were next asked to build an EJ action campaign similar to the tap water ad (chapter 4) and CSO PSA (chapter 5) projects completed earlier in the school year. Students were again given a menu of options and project formats to demonstrate their understanding. As detailed before, in the interests of ensuring the amount of work assigned to each group was equitable, each option—whether creating a skit, commercial, hand-drawn poster, or website—was awarded a certain number of points according to the size of the group completing the work product.

As groups began transitioning from being researchers to being creators, I also attempted to inspire them to become activists. Taking an entire class period, I would share past examples of exemplary work from previous years' EJ Expos. I loved sharing these past exemplars. It not only happened to be a lot of fun taking a walk down memory lane but, more importantly, it helped my current students dream about what they wanted to do for their projects and allowed them to gauge the level of content mastery and craftsmanship expected.

While we viewed previous years' creative and inspirational projects, I provided each student with a scoring rubric and a list of criteria that needed to be satisfied. Feeling inspired and a bit of pressure from the approaching deadline, students got to work attempting to produce an early rough draft (typically only after a few days of work time). This early first draft approach encouraged students to move from project ideation (where many groups can often get stuck) to action, gently forcing them to synthesize and put their newfound background knowledge to work.

The fact that students had to prepare a draft and present their ideas in front of their peers also gave me a better understanding of which ones were experiencing success and helped me identify those needing additional scaffolds or support. Early drafts also served as inspirational motivators. Students who had been focused internally on their own projects were now exposed to the ideas and creations of their peers. Each draft was also critiqued, and the rubric-based feedback that each group received could be used to generate short-term goals to be pursued as soon as the next class period.

As projects moved from draft to finished product, preparing students for the EJ Expo became critical. This meant that a day or two before our celebration of learning, WE ACT staffers returned to the classroom for a mock expo—a preparation process akin to a dress rehearsal. During this essential preparation period, students set up their projects around the classroom as they would be displayed on the night of the event in the school's cafeteria. Doing so allowed students to practice what they would say to their audience and think strategically about how they wanted to arrange their work products, giving them one last chance to receive feedback and revise their work.

Finally, after becoming experts on their EJ topic and continually revising their work to address critical feedback they received, students were ready for expo night, which would be held in the school cafeteria. That day, in the class periods leading up to the moment when the cafeteria doors would open to the invited guests—classmates, teachers, administrators, family members, and local elected officials—a tension filled the air as students made one final push to prepare their projects for the public. During this last preparation period, I sat with each group. I did my best to provide last-minute suggestions and help troubleshoot any issues (primarily dealing with digital technology) that would inevitably arise. In the closing moments of each period, I told my students I was proud of all they had accomplished and encouraged them to enjoy the evening.

Immediately following the end of the school day, just a few hours before the EJ Expo, I would meet WE ACT staffers in the school cafeteria to set up for the night ahead. Our preparations would begin by wiping down and then relocating the cafeteria's tables, later serving as the display location for student projects. A few of these tables would be positioned side by side and become the resting spot for a buffet of traditional Dominican fare, its presence a straightforward way for my students and those in attendance to have their culture represented and connected to our academic work.

With cafeteria arrangements almost complete, students would begin to trickle in. After finding their table assignments, each group would set up their project materials, nervously chatting with one another as they waited for the guests from the community to arrive. Despite being given the same overarching task—educating and advocating for environmental justice—each project and table would look slightly different. The intentional flexibility and multiple pathways for students to demonstrate their understanding were on full display. And while many tables would have laptops set up—one propped open with a digital poster display and another connected to headphones so guests could listen to and watch a pre-recorded video, for example—other tables had trifold posters on view, like those found at a traditional science fair. Regardless of how projects were displayed, the transformation of our school cafeteria into an expo space made for a beautiful sight worthy of celebration.

Before the EJ Expo officially began, students were served dinner by WE ACT staff—the food's familiarity helped to settle their nerves and provide energy for the night ahead. Filling their plates high with food, students feasted on Dominican delectables like *pernil* (slow-cooked pork), plantains, spaghetti, salad, *moro*, and its cousin, rice and beans.

As food disappeared from plates and time ticked ever closer to the expo's opening moments, I would meet with a group of volunteers who had agreed to be judges. Drawn from a network of WE ACT's EJ advocates, the judges had the unenviable task of identifying the evening's top projects and were responsible for assessing the quality of each via the same rubric students had been introduced to in class. In this way, the expo was not just a celebration of learning but also a competition, adding an extra element of rigor and further pushing students to put together their best work and be their best selves in their presentations to the audience.

Preparations complete, the cafeteria doors would swing open, and the expo would be underway. A buzz of energy would fill the room as students waited anxiously for their first guest at their tables. At the moment when most of the audience had filled the cafeteria, I would step back to watch from afar.

Looking around, I saw students utilizing all the presentation skills they had practiced and honed throughout the school year, demonstrating that they had internalized how to communicate their ideas effectively to an outside audience. Energetic voices and hand motions would direct the visiting guests to an exciting statistic displayed on a poster board or an original photo in a digital display. I would see students rising to the occasion, asserting themselves as experts, exuding confidence and joy. Guests nodded their heads as they listened to student presentations, asked intelligent questions, and smiled as they viewed polished work products.

The EJ Expo and the judge's evaluations underway, I would sneak down to the school's auditorium to set up for the second half of the night's programming. There, in the silence of an auditorium soon to be filled with noise, a podium, microphone, and set of speakers would be arranged to amplify the voices of our student MCs and keynote speaker. With the setup complete, I'd head back to the cafeteria to catch the closing moments of student presentations and then kindly direct those assembled toward the auditorium.

When students and guests had finished creakily settling into their seats, the second half of the expo's programming would begin. Two students who had volunteered to serve as hosts for this portion of the evening's programming (a great strategy to incorporate and develop youth leadership practices) would rise and take the stage. Before expo night, each had rehearsed a script of opening remarks, and they now used their preparation and training to introduce the expo's keynote speaker.

Over the years, the guest who gave the keynote varied (some years it was a WE ACT staffer, while others it was a local EJ advocate). However, regardless of who spoke that evening, their message was inevitably the same: only together can we address environmental injustice in the community. For my students, who had just spent weeks becoming experts on and now advocating for environmental justice, this message was essential, as it not only addressed past class projects or ideas that had failed to come to full fruition but demonstrated to them what a long-term commitment to addressing injustice in their community looked like and could become, whether as a professional pathway or a realized dream.

As the keynote proceeded, judges—still upstairs—deliberated. With students and guests gone, the silence of the cafeteria provided them the space to revisit and discuss what they had seen and heard. Not wanting to influence opinions one way or the other, I would remain in the auditorium, waiting for one of them to hand me a slip of paper with the expo's winners. Once we had a decision in hand, WE ACT staffers and I would rise to the auditorium's stage, share a message of gratitude, and reveal the top projects.

First, we would recognize a few groups that had been granted honorable mention. We would ask individual students representing their groups to stand from their seats, and as they received a resounding round of applause, smiles would spread across their faces. Next, we would take from behind the podium three gigantic checks—the same you might see presented at a sports arena or a fundraiser. These checks, representing cash prizes generously supplied by WE ACT, would be granted to the top three expo projects.

At this point, a buzz filled the room, followed by loud chatter from students as they realized what was happening. Students leaned forward in their seats, excitedly awaiting our announcement. One by one, the third-place, then second-place winners were announced, each bounding up to the front of the auditorium to an eruption of applause.

Finally, following a drum roll and subsequent pause for dramatic effect, the EJ Expo's winner was revealed. Once announced, the auditorium would go bananas as students cheered the champions, who sprinted to join the other top projects at the front of the auditorium stage. Interestingly, and to my pleasant surprise, each year's winning groups were often composed of students who did not necessarily receive the highest marks in the classroom. Realizing that my "top" students were not often awarded prizes by judges—a group of relative outsiders—forced me to reconsider my notions of what being a "good" student entailed and encouraged me to continue to design opportunities similarities to the EJ Expo in the future.

Once the night's festivities were complete, and each expo participant had walked away with a certificate of achievement, gift card, and WE ACT youth membership card, all were invited to enjoy red velvet cake back upstairs in the school cafeteria. Once again, WE ACT staffers graciously served those in attendance, sliding thick cake slices onto students' and guests' plates. And while most took their cake to go, promptly stepping out into the late evening air, WE ACT staffers and I lingered. Exhausted, yes, but no doubt proud of what we had accomplished and celebrated with students while pursuing environmental justice.

Although my class focused on environmental justice, my approach to learning environment design can undoubtedly be applied to other school subjects. Indeed, I have seen firsthand how this curriculum design approach can be applied across different grade levels and content areas. What matters most is that it is centered on a learning-by-doing approach that allows students to build their background knowledge on locally contextualized issues, be supported by experts along the way, and be given opportunities to advocate for a cause in front of a public audience. And while it is undoubtedly helpful to teach at a school where an overarching framework like expeditionary, experiential, or project-based learning is actively being encouraged, supported, and pursued, it is also possible for educators working more independently to go it alone.

Indeed, when I showed up at a new school teaching a new course with little familiarity with the neighborhood in which I taught and the lived experience of my students, I intentionally started small. I began with a simple email inviting Ogonnaya to join me and my students in the classroom. From there, her initial visit organically grew into a long-standing collaboration with enormous impact. These sometimes serendipitous and always synergistic steps not only proved to me what is possible in the classroom but also filled me with an immense gratitude—for the willingness of organizations like WE ACT to work with young people in the local community; for open-minded colleagues ready to embrace new ideas; and for my students' inherent brilliance and eagerness to put their work on display for the betterment of their community in pursuit of environmental justice.

CHAPTER 8

Shifting Baselines and Gazes

A Focus on Hyperlocal Learning

When students walked into my classroom, I expected them to flip open their laptops and begin working on the warmup for the day's lesson. Having fully embraced our technological world, I felt it was essential to digitize all my daily assignments to harness the power of being connected to online resources and to give my students the tech skills they would need as they continued their educational journeys.

Recognizing and embracing this essential learning tool well before student laptop use in the classroom became ubiquitous meant that I spent considerable time writing grants and raising funds to ensure that all my students had access to a laptop when they entered the classroom. (Thank you, DonorsChoose, the teacher-uplifting organization dedicated to connecting classrooms to funders for trips, supplies, and more.) Initially, this 1-to-1 device-to-student ratio that existed in my class was an anomaly, despite my under-resourced school's best efforts to invest in tech. It was not possible to provide every single student at my school with access to a device, and that remained the reality until the COVID-19 pandemic made it an educational necessity that each student be able to connect to the internet at home. Unfortunately, but perhaps not surprisingly, given the nature of funding for schools serving low-income communities, it took a crisis to spur the district-wide adoption of one device for every student.

My students wholeheartedly adopted the use of devices in my classroom. In fact, immediately after students crossed the threshold out of my classroom into the hallway (and let me be honest, even while they were still in the room), they dug into their pockets or bags and began scrolling through their phones to catch up on texts and social media updates.

I mention this here not to fault educators or students for our collective attachment to and dependence on devices but to note their ubiquity. While the consequences and potential harm that our society and the educational landscape's reliance on devices continue to be researched and debated, the reality is that digital screens in the classroom are here to stay. As a life and environmental science teacher who wanted to engage and encourage students to appreciate the natural world, I had to get them outside the classroom, away from their devices, and into their neighborhood's learning environment.

Immersing my students in their environment was also a way to counter the ecological concept known as "shifting baselines," or the idea that as habitats are degraded or destroyed, each successive generation uses the current state of their environment (or the one they grew up knowing) as a reference point for what subsequent conditions should look like. Classic examples of shifting baselines include the extinction of passenger pigeons that once flocked together so densely that they darkened the sky, the extirpation of wolves from much of the western United States, and the near vanishing of salmon once so plentiful during their annual migration up rivers it was said that you could walk across their backs. And while there have been some, albeit too few, environmental success stories (the reintroduction of wolves being one of them), the overriding concern is that each generation, without having had direct experience living in a biodiverse world, will not know what came before them.

For students like mine, who live in urban centers, the reality of a shifting baseline was particularly acute because their environment had long been hardened into a jungle of concrete and steel. This meant I had to think of and create novel ways for students to interact with their environment. I had to engage them in a different kind of shift—a shift of their gaze.

In neuroscience, a gaze shift is "the realignment of the line of sight so as to bring the image of a new object of interest to the central retina where receptor density and hence visual resolution are the highest."[1] Applying this concept to my classroom, I purposefully designed and exposed my students to a learning environment that encouraged them to shift their gaze away from their ordinary routines (and screens) and bring the natural world into full view. One could even argue that inducing a gaze shift is, at its core, an overarching aim of education. It is the light-bulb moment. The emergence from Plato's allegory of the cave, serving as a window into new worlds and perspectives that can cause transformational changes in what students know and can do.

My preferred way of encouraging a gaze shift was to leave the classroom behind and immerse my students in the remaining green spaces of the city blocks around our school and park across the street. I loved asking my students to engage with the environment in this way. Doing so encouraged them to look at the world around them differently. It allowed them to act as practicing scientists, collecting hyperlocal data in their own "backyard" and contributing to the larger scientific community.

Students as Scientists: Street Tree Census

One of my favorite activities for intentionally shifting my students' gaze was teaching them to identify and assess the health of the trees growing on the blocks surrounding our school. This annual activity was an outgrowth of one particularly memorable learning experience that saw my students become officially trained, equipped, and outfitted by the New York City Parks Department during its decennial street tree census. The census, which relied heavily upon the volunteer efforts of everyday residents, mapped, identified, and assessed the health of every single street tree living along the city's streets. In turn, the data was used by the Parks Department to make informed decisions about where to plant more trees, direct arboreal care, and create a publicly accessible map that people could use to learn more about the trees in their neighborhood.

During the tree census, my students set out from the classroom dressed in bright green vests with tape measures and tablets in hand (alas, a full escape from screens is not always possible). Then, using the training they had received from the Parks Department, they collected and input various tree-centric data, including species name, trunk diameter, and general health, into their mobile device.

As they collected data, it was common for students to converse with community members who were curious about what they were doing. This meant that students could teach and further solidify what they had been learning by sharing it with their neighbors, spreading the gospel on the benefits of trees to all who were willing to listen.

For the next few days, my students continued to collect, input, and share their assessment of street trees around our school's neighborhood, shifting their gaze from the concrete sidewalk to roots, trunks, branches, and leaves. Before long, students who just a few class periods before didn't realize that trees came in different species could now easily distinguish a London plane tree from a Japanese zelkova and a Callery pear from a honey locust. By the end of the census period, my students-turned-community scientists had mapped the location, type, and health of hundreds of trees across dozens of blocks in the neighborhood.

Seeing how my students' gazes had shifted from their screens to the sightlines of silver maples—gaining ecological knowledge, learning data collection skills, and having a lot of fun—I set out to replicate the once-a-decade census as an annual event in my classroom. In subsequent years, I would spend a few days teaching students about the ecological and economic benefits (often referred to as "ecosystem services") of street trees and provide them with Parks Department–inspired training on how to use field guides to identify species, use a tape measure, and assess health problems on paper data sheets. Once trained, students would then take their newly learned skills outside and apply them to the trees on the school's block.

Working in pairs, students would first use their field guides to identify a tree (more than a dozen unique species were located directly around our urban school). Then, they would measure the trunk's diameter with their tape measures and, finally, record any observable problems (broken branches, exposed roots, damaged trunk) before making a final health assessment (good, fair, or poor).

For each tree, they repeated these steps, and by the end of a class period, students who had likely given little thought to the trees they passed every day outside their school were now aware of the variety of life around them.

Back in the classroom, students would enter their data into a shared class spreadsheet, compare it to the tree-census online map (along with previous years' class data), and analyze how the health and size of the trees they studied had changed over time. In this manner, the spirit of community science that made the street tree census possible could live on in my classroom every year and serve as a reference on the health and growth of the trees in our neighborhood.

A few years after continuing this modified version of the street tree census and seeing how it provided my students with community science opportunities, I wondered if there was a way we could extend our work beyond the blocks surrounding our school. My students, too, who were enjoying being outside and collecting data as urban foresters, also seemed to be curious if there were other means by which they could interact with nature in our neighborhood. Many of my students, who had spent their whole lives walking by urban flora without much thought, now wanted to know if there was something they could do to care for the trees affected by the litter frequently strewn across their roots and the plastic bags dangling from their branches. Hearing this and wanting to do more, I thought perhaps it was time to shift our gaze once more and extend our community science efforts to the park across the street.

Interdisciplinary Ideations / Science + History / Highbridge Park

Highbridge Park is a sliver of green space hugging the eastern edge of northern Manhattan. Steeply sloped and challenging to develop, it has remained relatively wild and serves as a reminder of Manhattan's verdant past. Once contiguous and a destination location for city residents looking to escape New York's bustling and cramped downtown, the park can feel like a disconnected and forgotten natural space today.

Decades ago, the power-hungry city planner Robert Moses rammed the Trans-Manhattan Expressway directly through the Washington Heights neighborhood, where Highbridge Park and my school were. While the new roadway allowed cars and commuters to easily bypass the city grid (when they weren't stuck in traffic), the thoroughfare and its clover-leafed exit ramps transected Highbridge Park into a series of difficult-to-connect patches of green.

The favoring of commuters over the local community, combined with the slow-moving train wreck that was city-wide disinvestment in public green spaces, ultimately led to the decline and disarray of Highbridge. The park became a dumping ground for trash, litter, used syringes, and old car parts. Encampments of the unhoused took hold beneath underpasses. Before long, people from the community stopped visiting Highbridge, deeming the park unwelcoming and unsafe.

In addition to the challenges that sprang from a car-centric culture, successive waves of immigration and human migration to New York City brought new species of plants. Once introduced, these non-natives (the flora, that is) often became invasive, disrupting every ecological niche. Ubiquitous patches of low-lying mugwort and garlic mustard plants dominated the understory, vines of porcelain berry ensnared and choked trees, multiflora rose bushes intruded upon trailways, Norway maples prevented light from reaching the forest floor, and thickets of Japanese knotweed densely congregated upon the park's steeply pitched slopes, decreasing biodiversity by outcompeting native New York flora and leaving the park more susceptible to future environmental degradation.[2]

In the mid-1990s, however, recognizing the dire need for the care of the city's green spaces and the diamond in the rough that was Highbridge Park, Bette Midler's New York Restoration Project (NYRP) established itself as the park's de facto caretaker. Supplementing and, at times, even supplanting the role of the Parks Department, this small but mighty nonprofit sought to beautify green spaces in underserved communities like Washington Heights. In pursuit of this mission, the organization's staffers and volunteers hauled tons of trash from

Highbridge's hillside, cut back virtually every vine choking its trees, and restored many of the park's natural spaces.

Shifting the Gaze Toward a Neighborhood Park

Learning of NYRP's efforts, I contacted Jason Smith, the organization's northern Manhattan site director. Jason, with his salt-and-pepper beard that depending on the season varies in length from grizzled to full-on forester, along with his well-worn Carhartt work-wear outfits, certainly looks like someone who cares deeply about natural spaces.

Accompanying Jason's woodsman-like appearance is an incredible depth of knowledge about urban parks and a keen ability to relay to others the interconnectedness between humans and the environment. While Jason was initially hesitant about working with my class—as he was used to relying upon adult volunteer efforts to aid NYRP's task of maintaining Highbridge—I am incredibly grateful that we had the opportunity to craft a curriculum together for the classroom.

After weeks of communicating with Jason, the plan for my classes was to spend successive periods over a week or two visiting, working, and learning in Highbridge. This meant my classes would meet Jason or another NYRP staff member at a predetermined location in the park (a great strategy to maximize time in the field) and engage in stewardship efforts.

Despite their initial interest, my students' reaction to venturing past the playgrounds and basketball courts they frequented and into the forested sections of the park was mixed. For them, leaving behind the familiarity of the plateaued street grid of the neighborhood and descending into a steeply sloped and densely canopied forest transected by winding trails was a novel experience.

Many who had lived their entire lives on the blocks surrounding the park would remark, "I never knew this part of Highbridge even existed." Others openly shared grievances about having to walk any distance past the streets immediately surrounding our school. In these instances, I would always provide space to let students openly share their reactions to being in a new part of their neighborhood but balance the venting of their frustrations by asking them to think about how their involvement with NYRP might help them see their environment with new eyes and allow them to directly contribute to the improvement of the green spaces in their community.

Once NYRP determines a park location worthy of restoration, its workflow follows a consistent pattern: First, remove all litter. Second, clear as many non-native invasive species of plants from the area as possible. Last, restore the cleaned and cleared space with native plantings. NYRP introduced this cycle of removing litter, clearing invasives, and planting native flora to my students as they worked alongside the nonprofit in Highbridge.

As we worked in this manner, I quickly learned that tree planting was much preferred by students over litter and invasive species removal. This preference for planting is not hard to understand, as removing scattered litter and firmly rooted plants is hard, physically demanding, and dirty work (teachers, be mindful of your students' precious footwear), whereas planting a tree—not necessarily any easier—is much more enjoyable because of the genuine and tangible sense of accomplishment that comes from putting a living thing into an empty patch of soil.

If you've never planted a tree (or anything, for that matter) with young people, it's an activity you should put on your bucket list. Unafraid of sounding hyperbolic, I can honestly say that working elbow to elbow with students—young people with the bulk of their lives still ahead of them—to plant trees in the hopes of renewing a maligned urban forest not only nourished my soul but encapsulated everything I thought education could and should be.

Watching my students work together to dig holes on the steeply pitched slopes of Highbridge forest, gently massaging the root ball of a tree sapling before tucking it into the earth—audibly promising this living thing that they would come back and care for it in the future—was, in many ways, the manifestation of my call to teaching, fulfilling my desire to create a better and brighter world for my students and the community in which I served. While planting native trees was of particular importance and incredibly helpful in encouraging my students to continue to shift their gaze in the very urban world they inhabited, my hope and optimism truly peaked when Jason asked my classes to take part in the reintroduction of the American chestnut tree to Highbridge forest.

Interdisciplinary Ideations / Science + History / Restoring the American Chestnut Tree

The American chestnut, a fast-growing and utilitarian deciduous tree (think wood products like cradles, cribs, and coffins) once found throughout the eastern forests in the United States, became functionally extinct by the middle of the twentieth century due to the introduction of the pathogen *Cryphonectria parasitica*, a deleterious invasive fungus from Asia.[3] However, thanks to decades of breeding efforts and advancements in genetic research supported by organizations like the American Chestnut Foundation, a hybridized (Chinese and American) chestnut tree has been reintroduced to the original chestnut's ancestral range. Urban forests like Highbridge are also being used as reintroduction and research sites to study the newly created strains of chestnut. The hope is that the intentionally bred Chinese-American hybrid will be fungus-resistant and allow the tree to once again play an ecological role in the parks and forests of North America's cities.

When I shared my newfound knowledge of and appreciation for chestnuts with students, I was reminded of the importance of incorporating history into the science classroom. Indeed, examining the history of the American chestnut, once a keystone species, not only demonstrated to me how far my ecological baseline had been shifted (before working with NYRP, I was unaware of the chestnut's importance) but also reminded me that incorporating an interdisciplinary and history-focused approach into teaching science was valuable for providing students with context, subsequently deepening their connection to the content we were learning.

Hybrids on Highbridge's Hillside

My students, having learned the history of the American chestnut and their upcoming role in helping determine its next chapter, set out for Highbridge forest. NYRP, having kept the location of the study site secret from the public for the health of the hybridized trees and the integrity of the ongoing research, led our group through a series of secluded pathways running along the steeply pitched slopes of the park.

Reaching the already cleaned and cleared research and restoration site, a few dozen hybridized chestnut trees were waiting for us. Each tree, about a meter high and twig-like in appearance, looked delicate and vulnerable as it pointed toward the sky from its black plastic pot perched upon the hillside. Already knowledgeable and well versed in tree planting from their previous work in Highbridge, students got to work, digging a hole, gently removing the chestnut tree from its container, placing it in the ground, and tucking soil snugly around its base.

Before long, pencil-thin chestnut saplings could be seen silhouetting the slope of the forest, ready to face the pending and inevitable onslaught of *Cryphonectria parasitica*. This time, however, unlike their purebred American cousins, these hybrid trees, with their genetically renewed vigor, were well prepared to survive and even thrive.

Today, a few years after the saplings were planted, I am proud to report that the chestnuts my students planted are now over ten feet tall. They represent the impact that partnering young people with environmental organizations like NYRP can have not only on the lives of those living now but also on those soon to come, giving further credence to the saying that "the best time to plant a tree is twenty years ago, but the second best time is today."

From Restoration to Intensive Action

After participating in our annual street tree censuses and working to restore Highbridge Park, I began to witness what could happen when I asked my students to get involved in their local environment. Always wanting to expand what was possible for my students' learning environment, however, meant that I was forever on the lookout for additional opportunities to engage them outside of the classroom. So, soon after my school decided to temporarily freeze its regular class program and allow students to take one class, all day long, for an entire week to more deeply explore an interdisciplinary subject area (a scheduling modification called "intensives"), I began wondering how I could build upon the foundation that had already been laid and shift my students' gaze deeper into their surrounding environment.

Pairing with my history teacher colleague Erick Espin, a native of northern Manhattan who exudes cool and has an uncanny ability to build deep and meaningful relationships with students, we designed a weeklong interdisciplinary course centered on the environment and history of Highbridge Park. The course, dubbed "Restoring Highbridge," was an amalgamation of our combined pedagogical and philosophical approaches to teaching and learning. With his deep and personal experiences as an Afro-Dominican growing up in our school's community, Erick wanted to infuse our curriculum with his knowledge of past local events and ongoing policies, along with my desire to engage young people in the environment. The result was that when our planning was complete, Restoring Highbridge envisioned students learning the history of how the unjust environmental conditions in our school's neighborhood came to be (and were allowed to continue) and actively working to rectify them.

To increase the authenticity and engagement we hoped Restoring Highbridge would bring to our students, I leaned into my partnership with NYRP. Once again, after learning Highbridge's history, students followed the organization's tried-and-true method of removing litter, plucking invasive species, and planting trees. This time, however, thanks to the intensive structure of our course and the greater periods of time outside the classroom that it allowed for, students could contribute to more extensive restoration efforts including the reconstruction of forest trails. Our extended time in the field also allowed our classwork to spill out of the park onto the blocks surrounding our school, and by the end of the week, every street tree around our building had been pruned and provided with a fresh layer of wood chips by its trunk.

For a final and culminating assessment of learning, Erick and I asked students to envision and create a plan for what they wanted to see on the school block. Turning their week of work into a vision, students dreamed of more trees on the sidewalk, tree guards (protective fencing) for every tree pit, a redesign of our school's overgrown gardens, and even a plan to close the street and establish a pedestrianized plaza where they could eat lunch and hang out with friends.

For Erick and me, seeing students articulate their dreams demonstrated how the interdisciplinary lessons and partnership we had created encouraged students to envision a greener and more equitable future for their neighborhood. In reality, however, we were uncertain if they would ever come to fruition. After all, we knew that come Monday, when our school's program was "unfrozen" and student schedules returned to normal, we would be back to teaching our (no less intensive) regular classes, consumed with the challenges and rigors of the daily life of a teacher. Thankfully, however, Erick and I were not the only ones who had noticed (or participated in) the work our students had done or witnessed the dream they had envisioned.

A Tilt Shift of Momentum

As we were planning our Restoring Highbridge course, Erick and I were approached by Rayner Ramirez, a longtime community member who lived on the block across the street from our school. Rayner, a multiple Emmy Award–winning documentary filmmaker and, at the time, expectant father, had been attempting to get the neighborhood community board to address the unsavory conditions outside his home. He was tired of seeing drug users inject themselves and then discard their syringes on his front steps. He was fed up with the rat infestations created by the accumulating garbage and food scraps left behind on the curb by local street vendors. And he was frustrated that despite multiple attempts to raise awareness and call his local elected officials to action, no progress was being made.

Seemingly hitting a dead end and perhaps inspired by the name of his filmmaking company, Tilt Shift Media (a "tilt shift" is a photographic technique that can be used to bring new perspective to a scene by changing the image's focal plane), Rayner also shifted his gaze and his tactics by reaching out to six schools near his home, one of which happened to be the one where Erick and I taught.

After a meeting between Erick, Rayner, and me, during which Rayner vented his frustrations and outlined a vision for engaging young people in addressing the conditions in the neighborhood, we invited him to share his story with our students. During a block-by-block tour in which Rayner pointed out the issues he was concerned about, Erick and I saw his message resonate with our intensive class. On the tour, students shared with us and each other that they too witnessed the same neighborhood conditions outside Rayner's home during their daily commutes to and from school.

After observing how our students responded to Rayner's guided tour, Erick and I attempted to weave their issues of concern into our curriculum. That is why, near the end of our Restoring Highbridge week, both Rayner and our class were found working side by side to spread wood chips around the trees in our neighborhood and school garden. Seeing the progress we made in a few short hours on issues he had been trying to address for months, Rayner continued building momentum.

As Erick and I turned our attention to our regular class program, Rayner began working behind the scenes to keep things going. After connecting with a group of six students interested in continuing the work they had been a part of with the Restoring Highbridge intensive, he invited them to share their vision for the future with the local community board.

At the meeting, students used photographs to show board members the beautification efforts they completed with Restoring Highbridge. They shared community-based survey data tracking quality-of-life concerns that they had collected with Rayner at a neighborhood street fair. Closing their presentation with a call to action, the six students implored the board to support them and their efforts for a cleaner and greener community.

When the presentation ended, the small audience at the meeting and the community board members seated at the conference table in the front of the room rose from their seats and applauded (a rare

deviation from ordinary board meeting proceedings). Upon returning to their seats, the board proposed that they draft an official resolution to recognize and support the work of the student presenters.
Adding to the surprise of the board's favorable response, a doctor
from a local hospital and a director from a local nonprofit attending
the meeting that evening pledged monetary support to help the student presenters continue their neighborhood beautification efforts.

News of Rayner and the six students' success at the community
board meeting spread quickly around our school, soon catching the
attention of the in-house nonprofit Futures Ignite. FI, whose mission
is to provide marginalized youth with leadership-building opportunities as well as college and career support, saw the response of those
at the board meeting as just the beginning of the fulfillment of the
students' vision, and sought to set ablaze the spark of interest that
was kindled.

Igniting the Future

The youth-led group, now expanded and empowered by the backing
of FI, soon began giving similar presentations to other community
board committees and even the local state senator. Soon after, additional pledges of monetary support from government officials, and
several successful FI grant proposals made the students' dreams a
reality. Thanks to the financial support it received, the students' vision, now dubbed the Clean Air Green Corridor (CAGC) project,
was soon supported by a full-time FI educator.

The following school year, the work and vision of creating a temporary pedestrian plaza for the students in Washington Heights was
led by the inspirational Génesis Abreu, who, like Erick, is a native
resident of northern Manhattan and a champion for social justice. As
a senior manager at FI, Génesis coordinated and led year-round social and environmental justice programming with dozens of students
working as community scientists, collecting data in the summer
from the forest of Highbridge and, during the school year from the
streets of the CAGC. With Génesis, students also completed weekly
litter cleanups after school with the Stewardship (STEW) Crew (in

partnership with NYC H$_2$O and with additional help from Erick) and continue to present their work and build a coalition of like-minded advocates.

In acknowledgment of their scientific and beautification efforts, students are paid small stipends, which has helped to fuel them to write op-eds for local publications, teach their peers about environmental injustice, install protective tree guards and planters along the block outside their school, host daylong youth-centered block parties closed to traffic, and engage in initiatives that speak to the power of what can happen when educators and their partners provide young people with opportunities to focus on their local environment.[4]

While all the efforts noted above are worthy of an in-depth retelling, there is one initiative in particular that I wish to highlight. I do so not only because I am fortunate enough to continue to be involved with it today but also because of its potential to serve as a model for others seeking to do similar work in their communities. The effort, known as the Green Corridor Lab: A Youth-Led Community Science Initiative (or GCL, for short), provides high school students opportunities (and stipends) to learn about and become directly involved in bettering their environment.

The GCL, composed of eleventh-grade youth leaders, meets after school for a year to collect data on their neighborhood's environment. Following an intentionally designed environmental justice–centered curriculum, they become community science experts (and advocates) for their community. Toward the end of each year, in recognition of their work and to realize the original six students' Restoring Highbridge dream, they teach their classmates all they have learned in a celebration of learning.

Breaking into groups, each GCL team designs lessons on air quality, open and green space, sanitation, or extreme heat, then proceeds to hone them for maximum effect over multiple rounds of feedback and rehearsal. Once finalized, the lessons are delivered multiple times during a daylong "environmental justice teach-in" to a cohort of younger students. By the end of the teach-in, an entire grade level has heard firsthand accounts of the environmental injustices in their community.

Recognizing that simply educating their peers about the CAGC and environmental injustice will get them only part of the way toward their vision of making a positive difference in their community, GCL youth leaders also invite their classmates to advocate along with them for change. At the close of the day, GCL presenters ask student cohorts and an advisory teacher to develop a community action project that identifies and researches a local environmental or social problem, collects and analyzes data, takes action, and presents what they have completed. In the past, this integrated approach—a call to action infused with a scientific method–supported framework for learning—has inspired students to investigate environmental issues like the impact of pollution on organisms in Highbridge Park and social concerns like the school-to-prison pipeline. Regardless of which topic students choose, the leadership of GCL student participants, who perhaps sense that they too can shift the gaze of their peers, is an essential component in each justice-focused initiative.

Today, thanks to the brilliance of GCL youth leaders and the support they receive through the tireless efforts of Futures Ignite staff, a clearly defined pathway exists for the entire school community to take part in CAGC initiatives that confront and take action on environmental injustice. And while the original Restoring Highbridge student dream of a permanent pedestrian plaza has yet to materialize, the CAGC's programming and progress toward helping it become a reality has nonetheless provided a great example of how seeking to shift the gaze can also begin to shift baselines back toward a more just and sustainable future.

Shifting Your Gaze

The interdependent stories I shared in this chapter are unique not only because they reconnect and shift students' gazes to the natural world but because of the hyperlocal flavor this approach can add to a classroom's learning environment. Indeed, all the stories I shared took place mere steps away from the front door of my school. And while the view from the top of the stairs at my school looked different from those of other educators at their buildings, the benefits of engaging students in their immediate surroundings, regardless of location, are clear.

Of course, there will always be bureaucratic, logistical, and safety-related challenges that accompany taking students outside the confines of a classroom's walls. However, wading through the red tape is worthwhile. Had I not asked my students to look differently at the trees on our school's block, we would never have ventured into High-bridge Park. Had we not helped restore the park across the street from our school, we would never have had the opportunity to be a part of the reintroduction of a near-extinct tree species. Had the planting of trees not demonstrated to me the joy students experience when they place a living thing into the earth, the vision of the Clean Air Green Corridor may not have taken shape. The point is that we, as educators, do not have to go far to bring the world to our students, and we do not necessarily need to have a visionary destination in mind when we leave the school building behind. Sometimes, where we are going is revealed to us along the way.

For educators interested in adding a hyperlocal learning element to their curriculum, I again suggest starting small. First, try using the school building surrounding the classroom as a place of learning. Perhaps begin by venturing into the hallway. Measure the physical space. Complete an energy audit. Reimagine how the walls and halls could transform into greener, more beautiful spaces. Build confidence. Lay a foundation.

Then, venture outside. Go for a class period. Host a Socratic circle in the schoolyard. Create an artistic sketch or compose a nature journal entry of whatever may catch your students' eyes. Write an ode to the natural world. Demonstrate a proof of concept for learning in and from the community. Then, go (just a bit) further afield. Along the way, pay attention to what your students (and you) enjoy, continuing to pursue organic and authentic connections between the hyperlocal community and the now-expanded walls of your classroom.

CHAPTER 9

The Classroom Is Your Oyster

Actualizing Educational Philosophies and Frameworks

Any teacher interviewing to secure a position at a school has likely been asked to share their educational philosophy—often described as a "teacher's compass"—providing direction on how to shape learning experiences and environments for students. My educational philosophy, which centers on creating local, authentic, and interdisciplinary learning-by-doing experiences for students supported by a community of experts, was also informed by the empirically grounded theoretical framework that I utilized for my dissertation.

To build my "theoretical frame," which can be thought of as a research study's guardrails, I drew upon the ideas of hybridity theory and the third space posited by the postcolonial theorist Homi Bhabha and built upon by urban geographer Edward Soja. Combining the ideas of these two theorists I came to understand the third space as being the tension-wrought location (social and/or physical) where two disparate cultures intersect. Seeing this intersectional space as a place of opportunity, Bhabha, whose work is grounded in the hegemonic practices of a colonizer and their impact on the colonized, posited that if the environmental conditions were right, disparate parties could find common ground and come away with a new appreciation for one another.[1] Using Bhabha and Soja's theorizing as my framework's starting point, I then followed the academic trails of science education researchers in their adaption of hybridity theory and the third space for their respective studies before applying a similar lens to my own.

The study I designed sought to determine if and how learning environments influenced a student's attitude toward science. Using a mobile science lab called the BioBus, whose mission is to provide high-quality science education experiences to young people from underrepresented communities, as the setting for my research, I made observations, conducted pre- and post-surveys, and interviewed students. My research determined that a BioBus experience, which I likened to a third space thanks to its ability to bring together the disparate worlds of practicing scientists and urban students, helped young people attain a more positive attitude toward science in one class period.[2] In turn, this finding inspired me to incorporate a third space lens into my own educational philosophy.

Back in the classroom, in an attempt to turn philosophy and frameworks into tangible classroom practices, I sought to construct third space learning environments that connected science to the lived experience and interests of my students wherever and whenever possible. That is why when Erick Espin and I were presented with the opportunity to co-design another week of "intensives" (chapter 8), I saw it as an opportunity to utilize my third space "teacher compass" to curate the curriculum.

In the process of crafting our curriculum, Erick and I decided that the intensive model, which allowed our class to deeply explore a topic for an entire week and get out of the school building, was an excellent way for students to gain a new appreciation for science, history, and an aspect of the natural world—in this case an organism they might otherwise not relate to. That is why, for the entire intensive week, Erick and I led our students on a deep dive into the history and scientific importance of *Crassostrea virginica*, or the bivalve more commonly called the Eastern Oyster.

Pursuing Professional Development: The First Shuck

My fascination for oysters and inspiration for using them to craft curriculum and a third space–informed learning environment was sparked during a professional development course I attended as a fellow at Math for America (MfA), an organization dedicated to supporting and celebrating science and math teachers. During a compelling MfA professional development course, I was lucky enough to learn from and with BioBus and the Billion Oyster Project (BOP), an organization with the goal of restoring 1 billion oysters to New York Harbor by 2035.

Using oysters as the driver of the professional learning experience, I, alongside my MfA colleagues, became immersed in the science and history of *Crassostrea virginica* over three workshops. The professional development course, hosted at one of BioBus's community labs, exposed me to oysters and the research-grade equipment scientists used to examine them. Oysters, which I learned are ecosystem engineers capable of filtering up to fifty gallons of water a day, are organisms I previously had little regard for. However, after the first BioBus/BOP workshop session, my attitude toward them would be forever changed.

The course's first session began when a BioBus community scientist shucked a live oyster and illuminated its flesh upon the stage of a stereomicroscope. The microscope, which was attached to a high-resolution camera and digital display, revealed the entrails of the mollusk. While a BioBus staffer respectfully and deftly probed the bivalve's body systems, I watched in awe at its still-beating heart, fully engrossed by its shimmering and trembling beauty. Seeing the inner machinations of a still-living oyster, combined with my newly gained background knowledge, inspired awe and motivated me to share similar experiences with my students.

On another evening of the workshop, my commitment to bringing oysters into the classroom was further cemented. The professional learning experience, which entailed trekking over the busy FDR highway and visiting a park next to New York City's East River, allowed me to watch BioBus and BOP staffers hoist an Oyster Research Station (ORS), a heavy, plasticized black metal cage covered in muck, out of the river and onto a landing where my MfA colleagues and I had gathered.

With the ORS still dripping the estuarine waters of the East River, a BioBus scientist removed the bungee cords holding the sides together. Peering down into the now-exposed interior of the ORS, I tried to get a better sense of its contents. As I observed, a BioBus scientist bent down, brushed away some muck, and pulled multiple clumps of living oysters out of the ORS. The oysters, representing an ecosystem in miniature form, had been intentionally placed in the ORS weeks ago by BOP to better gauge this location's potential for restoration.

The BioBus scientist started to shake the oyster conglomeration, causing a menagerie of living things to scuttle in and out of view. I caught glimpses of shrimp, crabs, and small fish, while also being drawn to the translucent globular bodies of sessile invertebrates like sea grapes and their more colorful cousins, chain tunicates, affixed to the hard surfaces of the ORS—wildlife wonders exemplifying the oyster's vital ecological role.

It was amazing to see how the reintroduction of one organism—the lowly oyster—that just a few years before was virtually nonexistent in New York waters could benefit many others. Witnessing the ecological Garden of Eden that is an oyster reef, even if it happened to be a miniature one contained within an ORS, was a celebratory occasion.

Perhaps catching wind of my spirited mood, our group, after returning the oysters and their companions to the ORS and the East River, gathered at a nearby oyster bar, where we clinked half-shells and drinking glasses in a toast to all that we had learned and the restoration of *Crassostrea virginica*.

Pursuing Professional Development: Preparing for Oysters in the Classroom

The next step I took to bring oysters into my classroom and create a third space–inspired learning environment was to become a certified BOP teacher. This entailed spending an entire day on coincidentally oyster-shaped Governors Island, a short ferry ride south of the tip of Lower Manhattan. On the island, a one-time US Army barracks-turned-carless park, sits both BOP headquarters and the famed Harbor School, a public high school founded to educate and train its students to become directly involved in restoring oysters in New York Harbor.

After successfully joining Harbor School students on their morning commute (the school is only accessible by ferry), a few other teachers and I, in pursuit of ORS training, were greeted on a landing dock by BOP educators. After a short walk across the island, Harbor School student guides led our group on a behind-the-scenes tour, and after viewing a series of classrooms, we entered BOP's aquaculture lab.

Stepping into the lab, I was immediately struck by the presence of a series of tall aquarium-like columns tinted with different algal-colored shades ranging from bright green to yellow to brown. Next to the columns, whose algal contents are used as oyster food, our group gathered around an enormous, shoulder-high blue plastic tub containing dozens of shells peppered with oyster babies known as "spat." The spat, which Harbor School students were carefully culturing for their eventual release into New York Harbor, were a visible representation of the seriousness with which BOP took their restoration efforts.

After our tour, I spent the rest of the day becoming certified to use BOP's curriculum and associated scientific equipment. The hands-on training process, which allowed me to become intimately familiar with BOP's harbor restoration approach and practices, provided insights and inspiration on how to support my students as community scientists. Gaining access to BOP's curriculum, resources, and staff also made it possible for me to help my students connect science to the city they live in and acquire the science and engineering practices championed by the Next Generation Science Standards with the added real-world benefit of helping BOP fulfill its mission of restoring oysters to New York Harbor.

Leaving Governors Island fully certified and with a deeper understanding of oysters, I was excited to bring them and the ORS experience into the classroom. And with the next iteration of "intensives" just around the corner, I saw a perfect opportunity to turn the mighty bivalve into a curricular keystone.

Interdisciplinary Ideations / Science + History / Pairing Oysters with Intensives

With my BOP certification complete, I sought to incorporate my training into my third-space educational philosophy. Viewing oysters and the work of marine scientists as two unique and potentially intimidating science-centered entities, I imagined that an intentionally designed intensives' curriculum could be an excellent way for students to get over any trepidation they might have and subsequently build new connections and learn from (and within) the environment around them.

Sharing my ideas with my intensive co-designer Erick Espin, I excitedly described how we could use the history and science of oysters in New York as a central case study for our curriculum. To his credit, Erick, despite being unfamiliar with oyster history and BOP, embraced the idea.

Soon after, we developed a plan to use Erick's expertise as a history teacher and my recently acquired ORS certification to build our students' background knowledge about the history of oysters in New York's waterways and engage them in BOP's ongoing restoration initiative. To teach oyster history, Erick used a series of historical photographs and Mark Kurlansky's *The Big Oyster: History on the Half Shell* as an anchor text to construct a narrative about the importance oysters played in New York City's history.

During precolonial times, New York Harbor was home to billions of oysters, whose beneficiaries were the local Lenape tribes. Colonial settlers also capitalized upon the bounty of half-shells, turning their plentiful presence into a seafood industry that made New York the world's oyster capital.

However, the good times New Yorkers experienced during the Industrial Revolution did not last. Over a series of environmentally deleterious decades, oysters and the harbor water quality to which they were inextricably linked declined precipitously. As oyster populations dwindled, their capacity to filter water was similarly reduced. This led to a vicious cycle of ever-declining oyster populations and water quality. Eventually, city officials became so concerned about New Yorkers being sickened by the consumption of raw shellfish from the ceaseless flow of untreated sewage into the harbor that they banned all oyster harvesting, effectively shuttering an entire industry and way of life overnight.

The near extirpation of the oyster population in New York waters had disastrous environmental consequences. Without oysters and the reefs their conglomerations constructed, the organisms that depended on them for food and habitat disappeared. In addition to this loss of biodiversity, the city shoreline became exposed. No longer was the water's edge protected by wave-attenuating oyster reefs, a fact made all too real by the flooding and damage caused by today's most powerful storms.

Despite the history of oysters being a depressing environmental tale, serving as yet another example of a shifted baseline, Erick and I knew it was essential to teach our students about the story of oysters to help them understand how their city's environment had changed over time. We also knew we did not want to dwell upon this disheartening environmental reality. Instead, we tried to instill within our students a hopeful message, and to do so, we shifted their attention (and gaze) to the local environment.

Localized Learning: Philosophies and Frameworks Combine

Leaving the classroom behind, our intensive class rode the subway to Manhattan's southern tip, hopped aboard the Governors Island ferry, and met up with BOP educators at their headquarters. Throughout the day, our students toured the same aquaculture lab I visited during my recent training and learned how to collect data from an ORS as community scientists. A bonus to their visit was the opportunity to climb upon vast piles of oyster shells—modern-day equivalents to long-lost Lenape middens. The massive mounds were a product of a partnership between BOP and the city's restaurants, diverting thousands of pounds of waste from landfills while aiding BOP's construction of artificial oyster reefs. Returning to our school that afternoon with a deeper understanding of bivalves and BOP, along with ORS building materials and a bucket full of live oysters, our students were prepared to explore a body of water closer to the classroom.

With ORS building materials stashed away in the corner of the classroom for later use and the live oysters we acquired happily eating algae in a small aquarium, we once again ventured outside. This time, Erick and I led our students through the twisting trails of Highbridge Park, emerging from the urban forest near the northern tip of Manhattan. Crossing the intersection of the Harlem River Drive and Tenth Avenue, we continued into Swindler Cove—one of the last remaining places on the island of Manhattan with a natural shoreline. And while it was tempting to linger upon this unique urban beach, the frigid temperatures and our obligation to reach our ultimate destination meant we had other matters to attend to.

As we left the shoreline, a BioBus mobile lab and one of the two community scientists operating it came into view. Seeing our group, she opened the mobile lab's door, beckoning us to enter. On this particularly frigid winter day, the yellow, orange, and powder-blue retro exterior of the transit bus-turned-science lab that had navigated its way to the confluence of a pier and seawall looked particularly inviting.

Students, perhaps too frigid to appreciate the full suite of the mobile lab's swagger, rushed to clamber on board. However, if they had taken a moment to examine it more closely, they may have noticed a series of solar panels atop its roof that, on a sunny day, provided enough power to charge the batteries stowed within the bus's interior. These power sources, which in part ran the lab's microscopes and digital displays, were accompanied by a small garden on the lab's roof and, under its hood, a diesel engine fueled by used vegetable oil. All elements combining to create a memorable example of sustainable science education.

The BioBus community scientists welcomed students inside the mobile lab with smiles that warmed the frost from their fingertips.

Looking around the bus's interior, which had been entirely gutted of passenger seats, students saw a series of stereomicroscope stations. Each scope, like those in the brick-and-mortar lab I had visited during my M*f*A course, was outfitted with a high-definition camera and connected to a digital screen. This unique and intentional design created a multimodal learning experience for students that encouraged them to discover, explore, and pursue our oyster intensive more deeply.

While students were getting accustomed to the mobile lab surroundings, one of the BioBus scientists and I somewhat begrudgingly left the cozy lab space to brave the cold. Pursuing our class's ORS, we walked a few short steps to the seawall, grabbed a long aquamarine rope, and hoisted the cage-like container onto the concrete with a thud.

With the excesses of the Harlem River's waters dripping off the black plasticized wire, we set to work to remove the bungee cable holding the ORS together. Once it was disassembled, clumps of oysters and other entrapped aquatic creatures were carefully cajoled into specimen containers and quickly shuttled back inside the mobile lab for examination.

Returning with our bounty to the mobile lab's interior, we spread the oyster clusters and other marine organisms onto the stages of awaiting microscopes. Soon after, students began their scientific exploration. Working in small groups, they flipped on the lights of their high-powered microscopes and were instantly transported, as I was only a few months before, into the world of the oyster.

These students-turned-scientists, now fully immersed in an oyster exploration in their own backyard, took turns making observations and asking questions about what they were viewing. Our team of instructors encouraged them to try to identify the species they were seeing, steering them toward copies of glossy field guides. While some groups continued to explore the contents of the ORS under their microscopes, another set of students made their way to the back of the mobile lab with oyster clumps in hand.

At the back of the bus, students used a metal probe to gently tap upon each bivalve's shell. If the taps felt firm and the oyster's shell was stuck together tightly, it meant it was alive and well. A squishy feel and hollow sound? Unfortunately, not.

Having meticulously recorded each oyster's survivorship in their lab notebook, students next used small calipers to measure each survivor's size as well as the mass of the entire mollusk conglomeration. As these measurements continued to be made, another group used water quality test kits to collect data about the conditions of the water, adding yet another layer to the BioBus data-collection experience. All elements of the BioBus-BOP exploration were in motion, and the students, who had known almost nothing about oysters just a few days before, were now actively working as community scientists.

With our ORS reassembled and its inhabitants safely returned to the water, Erick and I used the next few days to assess our students' understanding. Using the ORS materials we had brought back from BOP headquarters, students were tasked with constructing a model oyster reef with the idea that in the future it (along with the data we collected) might help the organization restore the waterway near Swindler Cove.

To help students construct their model reefs, we encouraged them to draw upon their understanding of oyster history and ecology as well as inspiration from their imagination. The result was model reefs that ranged from content-centric to borderline crazy. While some models looked similar to the ORS we pulled from the river, others took the form of sea walls or turreted medieval castles. Regardless of design, however, each model reef gave Erick and me a window into what our students had learned and how they viewed their participation in exploring their environment.

We celebrated our students' learning on our last day of intensives. To do so, we invited BOP, BioBus, and other colleagues into the classroom. Once everyone was gathered, students spread out around the room and passionately presented their oyster reef models to our visiting guests. As the clock ticked closer to the end of another intensives week, Erick and I provided our students with one last opportunity to get up close and personal with their topic of study.

Bringing students to the center of the room, we presented each with the chance to indulge in eating an oyster on the half shell.

Students, realizing what had been placed before them, reacted with various emotions. And while some shied away from the shucked seafood, others enthusiastically embraced the experience. Raising the bivalves to the ceiling, we acknowledged our students for their week of learning in the local environment and applauded them for their contribution as community scientists before those willing to indulge savored a final slurp.

This experience, driven by my third-space educational philosophy framework, was made possible because I chose to purposefully pursue professional development and tap into an incredible network of resources and partners. And while staying true to a course set by your teacher's compass is not easy, the reward for doing so can be the creation of powerful, meaningful, and potentially tasty learning environments connected to the natural world.

CHAPTER 10

Maps and Apps

Preparing Students for College and Career

One of my favorite moments as a teacher was when one of my former students would return for a visit. For me, these visits stirred a rare feeling of gratitude and accomplishment in a profession that can sometimes feel thankless. When former students returned, we would hug, high-five, smile, and sit down for a chat if the timing was right. While I was always grateful and appreciative for the opportunity to talk with former students, there were a few instances where the conversations that unfolded would transform my approach to education.

Every so often, a student will pass through a teacher's classroom who will forever be remembered. Whether it be their content mastery, work ethic, sense of humor, or joie de vivre, the presence and memory of that student becomes eternal. For me, one of those students was Joanna, who exhibited a maturity and sophistication that belied her age. And while it is true that she was a top performer academically, it was her intangible character qualities that truly set her apart from her peers. Joanna, who was involved in all aspects of our school, from student government to athletics, was quick to smile and share a laugh with a classmate. She picked students up when they were down and helped unite the school around common causes, leading rallies against gun violence, climate change, and educational inequities.

During the fall of Joanna's senior year, she was accepted into a prestigious higher-education opportunity program that recognizes top students from marginalized communities, matching them with an elite university and providing them with a full scholarship. It's an amazing opportunity and one that Joanna, like so many students from underrepresented backgrounds, both need and deserve, given persistent racial and socioeconomic achievement gaps.

The fall after high school graduation, Joanna, now enrolled in an elite college, returned for a visit. I was delighted to see her and interested in catching up on what I expected to be a seamless and impressive transition into college life.

Having navigated our obligatory greetings, I sat down with Joanna and asked how things were going—her response shook me to my educator core. Joanna shared stories of how she was not only struggling academically but also suffering from what she labeled as "impostor syndrome"—or the sense that she did not belong at the PWI (primarily white institution) she attended.

I reacted to this update with disbelief, empathy, and anger. Certainly, Joanna was not the first student I had taught to struggle with their transition from high school to college, but her incredible level of success at our school made it difficult for me to grapple with her genuine challenges. I thought, surely, if there was one student who could graduate from our school and hit the ground running in college, it would be Joanna. However, realizing this was not the case forced me to question my role as an educator and our broader education system.

Learning of the depths of Joanna's challenges reinforced my belief that American school systems and colleges need to do a better job supporting Black and Brown students, especially those graduating from urban school districts, which, to this day, are still bastions of segregation.[1] Even though elite colleges and universities tout their diversity statistics and vast support system for students from underrepresented backgrounds, Joanna's experience speaks to the need for additional resources to ease the transition between high school and college for our most marginalized youth.

As Joanna experienced firsthand, students like her who attend high schools in low-income communities are less likely to be exposed to a rigorous course load and more likely to attend schools underfunded and staffed by inexperienced teachers.[2] And while my colleagues and I worked relentlessly to provide Joanna and her class-mates with the best education possible, the truth was that our students did not have the same resources or support as those in more privileged locations.

This is not to say that students like Joanna are unable to be successful or even excel at the college level (she eventually graduated as a double major), but to draw attention to the fact that the playing field is not level and that we as educators, especially those of us teaching students from low-income communities, must yes, acknowledge this reality, and at the same time continually search for new ways to support the young people we serve.

Understanding the systemic inequities that persist within our education system, I embraced pedagogical practices that I thought would improve the learning environment in my classroom and better support and prepare students like Joanna for life after high school. I was constantly looking for new ways to make my classroom learning environment meaningful, relevant, engaging, and rigorous, providing ample opportunity for students to learn about science and the environment, develop content knowledge, hone essential skills, and prepare for their future. Sometimes, I conducted my search for continuous pedagogical improvement alone, but more often than not I saw the most powerful outcomes when I worked with a partner.

Partnering with Experts: Skills for College and Career

Joanna's struggles at college and her unpreparedness for the classes she took on campus left an indelible mark on me. That is why I was immediately intrigued when my longtime classroom partner, NYC H_2O, approached me with the idea of teaching students how to use an advanced data-mapping application tool that used the geographic information system (GIS).

NYC H_2O (also featured in chapter 3), an organization focused on educating the public about the environment and the ecology of New York City's waterways, was interested in bringing ArcGIS into my classroom. ArcGIS, an application more typically used by graduate students and professionals, can help users visualize an endless array of environmental data such as the changes of a landscape over time, the distribution of park space in a city, and the relationship between highways and air pollution. The learning curve required to use the application can be relatively steep, and without any firsthand experience using ArcGIS, I was skeptical about my ability to teach my students how to use the program. Thankfully, however, NYC H_2O was willing to guide me.

Aware that we were sailing into uncharted pedagogical waters, we decided to start small, developing an after-school pilot program that taught a self-selected group of students how to use ArcGIS mapping tools. However, we were convinced we were on the right track after viewing a compelling student-generated ArcGIS map from the pilot that overlaid historical and contemporary photographs to document gentrification and environmental injustice in the neighborhood.

That summer, I familiarized myself with ArcGIS by creating a map of my daily bike commute with StoryMaps, an ArcGIS web-based application. The tool combines data mapping and visualization with multimedia and text-rich stories. To construct my StoryMap, a multimedia, data-centric, interactive digital narrative about the environment, I dropped pin locations of landmarks along my commute, included images and video of the green spaces I passed through, and even inserted audio samples of noise-filled intersections I had to navigate. The experience of constructing my bike commuter StoryMap demonstrated to me how learning to use the application could teach students twenty-first-century skills and NGSS scientific practices, connect them to their local environment, and better prepare them for college and career.

Partnering with Experts: Co-teaching

After our successful pilot and my own self-taught ArcGIS experience, NYC H_2O and I collaborated to create a StoryMaps curriculum for the classroom. To support students on their learning journey and allow them to become proficient in using the application, we crafted a series of lessons that led students step-by-step through the StoryMap making process. This work, which saw me providing input on lesson agendas, learning objectives, and assessments, was supplemented by NYC H$_2$O's expertise in co-teaching StoryMaps in the classroom. Through the combination of these elements, students were soon utilizing the full power of the platform.

A typical week of teaching students to learn how to build a StoryMap started with a Monday visit by NYC H$_2$O. At the beginning of class, the organization's ArcGIS experts would introduce a particular StoryMap skill, such as adding images or audio through a short, direct-teaching (lecture-like) visual demonstration. Next, students would individually view a tutorial video and work to learn the skills taught within it by replicating a NYC H$_2$O–generated model StoryMap. Over the course of the next day and the rest of the week, students would gain proficiency with the skills they had been taught by applying them to their "My Environment" StoryMap—the overarching place-based project developed as an assessment tool for our curriculum. In this manner, week by week, students progressively mastered the various elements of StoryMaps, eventually producing a final My Environment map of their own.

The completed My Environment StoryMaps revealed a student's proficiency with using the software and served as a window into their local worlds. In one particularly memorable map, such rich details were provided that I felt I better understood who my student was and how they interacted with their neighborhood. The StoryMap began with a timeline of my student's life from birth to the present—including academic accomplishments, family loss, and summer travel destinations, complete with dates and photographs of the people and places nearest and dearest to them. After this timeline, they made evident their passion for basketball, using various media attached to an interactive map to pinpoint the names and locations of favorite courts in the neighborhood. As I scrolled past the courts' locations, I was able to hear an audio recording of my student completing warm-up drills, punctuated by the audible bouncing of the basketball, making this portion of the StoryMap particularly memorable.

Also included in my student's My Environment project was a map that traced their commute to school and the locations of their favorite restaurants. Upon clicking on the pin locations of each restaurant, hunger pang–inducing menu items like the traditional Dominican breakfast of *mangu* with salami, eggs, and cheese would appear. Toward the bottom of the StoryMap, my student shared photos of the urban landscape, famous cartoon characters, and Dali-inspired artwork that they generated, along with neighborhood map locations of where they had been created, all combining to weave a powerful narrative for the My Environment project.

While this student's particular StoryMap was a standout, all the My Environment finished products revealed fascinating details and examples of how my classes interacted with and thought about the immediate world around them. And because this uniquely personal project was the first one completed in the new school year, it had the unintended benefit of helping me learn who my students were and what they liked to do. Capitalizing on what I can only describe as the ultimate start-of-the-year "getting to know you" icebreaker, I found myself returning to student StoryMaps multiple times (especially before the first parent-teacher conference) to help me establish and build the strong relationships essential for engaging students in the classroom.

Students as Scientists: Twenty-First-Century Skills and NGSS Scientific Practices

With the My Environment StoryMaps completed—and students having acquired a host of new mapping skills—I saw an opportunity to further prepare my students for the future. While some of my current and former students, like Joanna, were dynamic speakers and presenters already, I knew that many, if not all, would benefit from additional practice in communication. Indeed, proficient presenting and public speaking are two skills highlighted by the Framework for 21st Century Learning (Learning and Innovation Skills) and NGSS Scientific Practices (Obtaining, Evaluating, and Communicating Information). However, when my students gave in-class presentations, much was often left to be desired.

Without guidance on designing and delivering effective presentations, students defaulted to creating slideshows filled with a lack of visuals and an overwhelming amount of (very tiny) text. Standing in the front of the classroom, with their back often turned to their audience, students would commonly read what they had placed on each slide—verbatim. Having witnessed these lackluster presentations more than once, I designed templates with specific guidelines for students to use, along with suggestions for public-speaking best practices. While these foundational strategies helped improve student presentation skills, they by no means resulted in the level of proficiency I knew students needed to attain to be prepared for college and career.

With this overarching target in mind, accompanied by a shorter-term goal of preparing students to confidently and capably present in front of experts and the public later in the school year, I asked them to present their My Environment StoryMaps in small groups. This small-group approach was both time-saving and stress-reducing—time-saving because presentations could be completed in one class period, and stress-reducing because students, especially those who dreaded public speaking, were more comfortable sharing due to their familiarity with their (self-selected) group and the content of their presentations (themselves and their environment).

On presentation day, students entered the classroom and sat with their groups, taking turns displaying and presenting their Story Maps. NYC H_2O visiting experts and I circulated around the room, catching snippets of conversation. Passing by each group, we heard passionate presenters sharing their My Environment projects with an engaged and intently listening audience (students love talking and listening about the lived experience of themselves and each other). I was particularly impressed by those students who, earlier in our unit, had shared with me that they were uncomfortable presenting but were now enthusiastically sharing their projects with their friends. And even though students were presenting to familiar faces that they may have known for years, I still heard individuals remark, "I never knew you lived on that block," or, "I love visiting that park with my little brother too." These comments served as powerful testimonial of StoryMaps' ability to not only hone students' presentation and speaking skills but also allow them to make connections to each other and their environment.

Students as Scientists: From Acquired Skills to Actions for Advocacy

After the success of our first iteration of StoryMaps, I looked to reinforce my students' newfound skills so they could both internalize and subsequently draw upon them when needed. To do this, NYC H_2O and I asked students to examine and document the environment surrounding our school's blocks. Seeing a perfect opportunity to connect more students to the ongoing Clean Air Green Corridor (CAGC) project highlighted earlier in the book, I once again reached out to Génesis Abreu from Futures Ignite.

On the launch day of a new StoryMaps project, I invited Génesis from Futures Ignite into the classroom to share the story of the CAGC. During the visit, Génesis told stories and projected images of the neighborhood beautification and environmental justice work CAGC youth participants had completed. And while some students were already familiar with the CAGC project, most were hearing and seeing the ongoing advocacy efforts being carried out around their school for the first time.

Being made aware of their peers' actions in pursuit of a cleaner and greener environment did not automatically equate to my students thinking they too could similarly change the environment for the better. Indeed, many of them, having attended our school since middle school and seen little (if any) positive neighborhood change, vociferously pushed back against the notion. This openly shared disbelief, however, did not dispel the day's core message, and in many instances, Génesis even leaned into students' skepticism, both listening to and encouraging them to think critically about why their neighborhood was in a state of disrepair and subject to environmental conditions not evident in more privileged parts of the city. Although many students continued to be unconvinced about their ability to make the city more environmentally just, they at least began to consider the role they might play in helping to make the goals of the CAGC a reality.

Students as Scientists: Advocating for Change

Over the next few weeks, students, using the same StoryMaps skills they had learned in their My Environment project, set about to address the call to action Génesis left them with—namely, to document and advocate for environmental justice on the blocks surrounding our school. Working diligently inside and outside the classroom, students noted the hazards (and amenities) surrounding our school building, pinning the multimedia-centered evidence they collected to specific map locations.

When students' projects were finished, Génesis returned to our classroom for presentations, viewing student StoryMaps with titles like "Building a Resilient Tomorrow," "Power-Up for Change," and "The Future of the CAGC." Within each map was evidence of the unjust environmental hazards that could be found in the neighborhood, juxtaposed with uplifting calls to action. Students used inspirational quotes to draw attention to abandoned buildings, testimonials on the impact of walking by continually littered street corners, and uplifting images of the CAGC and its vision for a cleaner and greener future.

When I first set out to incorporate StoryMaps into my classroom's learning environment, I sought to address the genuine needs that my former students, like Joanna, faced when they graduated from high school. Indeed, at the time, it was my goal and belief that if students could acquire new skills and apply them by completing a rigorous task in school, they would be better positioned to utilize them in a college classroom or, one day, even in the boardroom. To reach this goal, I had to take risks by embracing new technologies—and gaining support from partners like NYC H_2O and Futures Ignite. And while the support I garnered from partners allowed me to address my initial desires to support my former, current, and future students, it also came with several other unexpected benefits.

Today, NYC H$_2$O and Futures Ignite continue to use ArcGIS mapping to support and guide the youth leaders of the CAGC and their dream of a cleaner and greener community, as well as an ever-growing number of STEM leaders and environmental justice advocates at other schools. This unintended multiplier effect speaks to the power of what can happen when we as educators take calculated curricular risks, equip ourselves with proper training, synergize with partners, and seek to meet the needs of students like Joanna.

CHAPTER 11

From Isolated Islands to a Connected Archipelago

A Cross-Classroom Approach

One of the most beautiful things about being a teacher is that when you literally or metaphorically shut the door to your classroom, the noise from the hall and the myriad demands of the system at large fade into the background. The presence of mind required to create a welcoming classroom environment conducive to student learning is all-consuming. In this way, a teacher's classroom is akin to a faraway island. An island that operates with its own norms, rules, systems, culture, and ways of being. In the best of times, this island and its environment can elevate the learning experience for all. However, because of the classroom island's inherent isolation, those lacking positive environments are fraught with danger and risk.

The island I tried to create inside the walls of my classroom was guided by an intentional blend of student interest and learning standards. I taught the curriculum via empirically based pedagogical best practices and a healthy mix of stagecraft and artistry. Over time, with reflective adjustments both before, during, and after each class, I learned what worked best for my students, and the island blossomed. Yes, it occasionally would be visited by dark and stormy weather, a frustrating miscommunication between teacher and student, or perhaps an unforeseen interruption to learning (*another* fire drill). On many days, however, because the preconditions were right, the island was full of sun and clear skies.

The relatively idyllic island where I spent my days was attractive, appealing, and comfortable. I would traverse the island with a cohort of student visitors, teaching the lessons I honed from year to year.

When the visitation time to the island had concluded, my visitors would depart, carrying their luggage on their backs to another nearby isolated piece of land down the hall.

Most days, I rarely ventured away from my island. I happily ate lunch at my desk watching a pair of pet turtles bask in the sun of the lab sink-turned-terrarium at the back of the classroom. Despite the sunshine and steadfast company of my shell-carrying friends, I would sometimes long for collegial connection and become curious about what was happening down the hall on all those other classroom islands, so close yet so far away. Before long, I would set off in search of new cultures, communities, ideas, and strategies.

I sometimes left my island to attend grade-level meetings or weekly professional development workshops with my colleagues. The most powerful ideas and practices gained from these departures, when implemented with fidelity, helped to connect our classrooms, improving our students' learning environment and experience across our archipelago. And while implementing new pedagogical strategies across our school was a net positive, this approach did not always address the siloed curricula housed upon each spit of land.

The downside to this curricular isolation is the disconnectedness (or culture shock) a student might feel hopping from island to island. What they are learning and doing in science likely has little to do with what occurs in history, English, or math. To rectify this disunity and unite our chain of disparate islands, it is necessary to take a cross-classroom interdisciplinary approach, where two or more teachers combine their courses and curriculum into one comprehensive learning environment akin to a bridged archipelago.

Bridging the Archipelago: Cross-Classroom Curricular Beginnings

Given the myriad challenges faced by the classroom teacher working on their own, it should come as no surprise nor be contested when I say that most educators have little time or energy to adopt a cross-classroom interdisciplinary approach. I found, however, that selectively searching for and embracing specific opportunities to do so not only improved my classroom practice but also created unique and meaningful learning opportunities for students.

Although observing colleagues and working with them to design curriculum is not often high on the list of recommended ways to pursue professional development, I found that these collegial experiences had an outsize influence on my day-to-day pedagogy. For one, my colleagues were intimately familiar with the context of where I worked and the students I taught, so we could more easily communicate and proactively address the needs of our current, former, and future students. This also meant that from time to time, we could work together to craft interdisciplinary curricula across our classrooms.

I loved working with my colleagues to design a cross-classroom interdisciplinary curriculum because it allowed me to deepen my content understanding of a subject area different from my own, and it provided me the opportunity to learn new pedagogical practices. Often, these collaborations led to my colleagues and me incorporating new or shared teaching routines and approaches that we agreed would work best for our students across our courses. No longer were our classrooms operating as isolated islands with disparate cultures; rather, they had become symbiotic learning environments sustained and reinforced by our interdependence.

Of course, saying you are interested in adopting a cross-classroom interdisciplinary approach is one thing, but doing so is something else entirely. And while it is easy to dwell on the logistical challenges that will most certainly arise when one pursues such an approach, many, if not all, of these obstacles can be confronted and overcome with the right partner(s). Luckily, for me, my first partner happened to be a masterful English teacher.

Anthony Voulgarides, a native Alabamian with a Southerner's soul and Northeasterner's edge, and I entered the teaching profession simultaneously through the same alternative certification program. We initially crossed paths the summer before our first year of teaching while attending a crash course in education, only to part ways to our respective placement schools and the challenges awaiting us as first-year teachers. Occasionally, we would rub elbows as we worked toward our master's degrees in education but did not join forces in an interdisciplinary capacity until more than a decade later when we both found ourselves teaching seniors at our school in Washington Heights.

As I was working with Anthony on the twelfth-grade team at our school, it became evident that he was passionate about imparting upon students his love for books and crafting powerful prose. Because of our different content areas, I did not initially consider Anthony to be a cross-classroom curriculum partner. Thankfully, however, my initial intuition was incorrect and Anthony, one of the most meticulous planners I have ever encountered, was the perfect complement to the more high-flying visionary approach to curriculum design I often employed.

Our interdisciplinary collaboration started when I tapped Anthony as the point of contact for the guest judges at one of the first Environmental Justice Expos (the annual celebration of learning hosted in partnership with WE ACT detailed in chapter 7). During a grade-level team meeting a few days after the EJ Expo, Anthony openly wondered (thanks to a supportive nudge from our school's administration) if there was a way we could use the culminating experience of the EJ expo to reimagine and redesign our students' senior spring. We both agreed that for the second-semester seniors only days away from graduation, a cross-classroom interdisciplinary project focused on the local environment might help keep them motivated and inoculated from contracting the proverbial "senioritis," a very real affliction.

We enacted our initial attempt to roll out a cross-classroom approach the following spring. In my classroom, I continued the environmental justice partnership and expo project I had established with WE ACT. At the same time, students worked on a synthesis essay in Anthony's English class and a community-based participatory research project in their civics course taught by our colleague Charlie Maciejewski. When we combined the classes, students, instead of focusing on three disparate topics in science, English, and civics, were now gaining a deeper understanding of one unifying content theme across three different classrooms.

While students still became experts and designed PSAs on an environmental justice issue they wanted to deeply explore in my classroom, their background knowledge was grounded in a broader exploration of environmental justice in Anthony's English class, where a variety of primary and secondary sources were used to answer the overarching question, "Who is responsible for protecting my environment?" in a cohesive argumentative essay (with a counterclaim and rebuttal).

Charlie further enriched our students' immersion in environmental justice by asking our second-semester seniors to become active community members. By providing resources for students to attend local board meetings, participate in WE ACT's climate justice advisory group, interact with city council members, collect survey data from community residents, and teach the elementary students from our school—opportunities I had always wanted to include in the environmental justice projects in my class but never had the time to do so—Charlie was able to increase the relevance, rigor, and authenticity of our collaboration.

Once our project was in motion, our triumvirate met frequently, providing each other with updates, troubleshooting logistical issues that would inevitably arise, and, most importantly, planning and preparing for the culminating Environmental Justice Expo. As our planning and student projects progressed, it became evident that adopting a cross-classroom approach encouraged more robust and higher-quality work products than those completed in years past. I was excited for them to be celebrated and shared with the public.

On the night of the EJ Expo, students engaged their audience in our school's cafeteria in powerful and nuanced ways. They spoke passionately about the environmental injustices they had studied. They beamed proudly as they told stories and showed visiting guests photos of themselves working in their community to draw attention to their issues of concern. It was clear to us as teachers that our students had internalized what they had been learning across our classrooms. We made this outcome possible because we adopted a cross-classroom interdisciplinary approach. And while our commitment to collaboration required additional planning and coordination to pull off, having the support of three teachers and a continuity of content across the subjects of science, English, and civics created the rigorous and high-quality final products we had envisioned in our initial grade-level meeting over a year earlier.

Reeling Before and From the Pandemic

Riding high off the success of our cross-classroom Environmental Justice Expo, Anthony approached me with a new idea to further deepen the burgeoning collaboration we had started. Having been recently awarded a substantial grant that would allow him to bring professional filmmakers into our school, Anthony wondered if we could use the same cross-classroom interdisciplinary approach and environmental justice lens to teach students how to make documentary films. I was immediately on board.

The following spring, filmmaking teaching artists from the Educational Video Center (EVC), a nonprofit that works with teens to produce social justice–inspired documentary films, were in my classroom. Cameras in hand, we led students outside on a brisk March day to practice capturing supplementary footage called "B-roll." Using the techniques that EVC educators had taught them, students panned, zoomed, and gathered a series of camera shots from various angles. Their excitement was palpable while documenting the raw conditions that caught their attention in the neighborhood. Overshadowing the kickoff of our new interdisciplinary collaboration, however, was the threat of our building's closure, and the very next day, the explosion of COVID cases across New York City shuttered the entire school system.

Having to adjust course abruptly, Anthony and I abandoned our filmmaking ambitions and, like thousands of other classrooms across the country, pivoted to remote learning. Reworking our previous year's cross-classroom collaboration, we fell back on the now familiar environmental justice PSA and synthesis essay, supporting students to the best of our ability to pursue a culminating virtual expo.

Choosing to follow the original cross-classroom project was a worthwhile decision. On a personal level, the necessity of collaborating with Anthony (despite the additional effort to do so) during an isolated time kept me connected to the collegial and family-like community of our school building, which I sorely missed. More broadly, the unequal and unjust COVID-19 health outcomes our school community was grappling with firsthand were an unfortunate yet stark reminder that what we were learning about in our classrooms mattered. Speaking eloquently during a final culminating virtual expo to an audience of over one hundred guests, our students shared their projects. They told stories of how learning about the environmental injustices in their community had asked them to look at their neighborhood in new ways and ask questions about how they could become active participants in solving them. And while Anthony and I were undoubtedly proud of our students' work, we also knew that our dreams of student-produced documentary films had been left unfulfilled.

A Yearlong Filmmaking Adventure

Toward the end of that year's summer, with the school year rapidly approaching, the pandemic still raging, the response to the murder of George Floyd ongoing, and our school cobbling together a plan for what a "normal day" would look like, I met with Anthony and the rest of the twelfth-grade team. To embrace our schoolwide "less is more" mantra, we decided to combine science, English, and Advanced Placement (AP) Research (a course that includes writing a twenty-page academic paper) along with an integrated co-teaching model (to serve those students who had an Individual Education Program, or IEP) into one yearlong course. Our thinking was that if students had fewer individual classes to manage, then the burden of having to learn during the pandemic might be eased. After much discussion, our team decided that the yearlong AP Research course would serve as the organizing force of our cross-classroom interdisciplinary attempt. Our mission? Teach students how to conduct original social justice–oriented research and collaborate with EVC to produce the documentary films that had been originally planned before COVID.

The project was as ambitious as it sounds, especially given what would come to be the stop-start, roller coaster–like nature of the school year. We had to contend with students who were remote, hybrid, and in-person, and continuously reassess our standards of academic rigor in the midst of the genuine trauma our students were facing, whether from coping with the death of a family member, a parent's loss of a job, or dislocation from home. Confronting these realities while trying to find time for ourselves and our respective families was (as I will share in a later chapter) overwhelming. Sometimes, our planning conversations became heated and, occasionally, exploded into confrontation. Reflecting on these circumstances now, I am not surprised. What we as a grade-level team were trying to accomplish—the creation of an interdisciplinary yearlong project across three classrooms with four different teachers, each with a distinct educational philosophy and unique pedagogical approach—was exceedingly difficult.

Despite the challenges we faced in our partnership and the ongoing, often traumatic struggles of the students we were teaching, I look back on the year as one in which I learned more from my colleagues than perhaps at any other point in my career. I learned how teaching students the fundamentals of writing and giving them ample time to practice and implement what they were learning was instrumental to helping them gain the skills and confidence necessary to write a twenty-page research paper. I gained a new understanding and appreciation for building relationships, watching and listening as a colleague on Zoom connected with students in the virtual classroom while living in COVID-19 isolation. I learned how to support and advocate for special education students who typically did not have access to or were commonly overlooked for enrollment in Advanced Placement classes. And I realized that the opportunity to work intimately with a group of professionals can markedly improve your teaching practices and ability to support the students you serve.

A Filmmaking Journey Fulfilled

Following an entire semester of our students researching and writing about a variety of social justice topics of their choosing, our four-teacher, three-classes-in-one interdisciplinary course invited EVC back into the classroom for the final months of the 2021 school year. EVC instructors, working closely with our teaching team, helped students learn the basics of documentary film production in person as well as on Zoom. Each film, centered on a student's social justice–focused AP Research project, was pieced together from mobile phone footage and school-supplied audio and video equipment. As one would expect, the isolating nature of the pandemic made student collaboration difficult. To our students' credit, however, they displayed incredible resilience and determination, capturing B-roll footage from the neighborhood surrounding our school and conducting interviews on Zoom with subject matter experts.

Slowly but steadily, students collected a body of documentary film evidence and then fashioned it into a compelling narrative that they fastidiously wove together using web-based video editing software. The films were then screened at another well-attended virtual expo at the close of the school year, with film topics ranging from housing affordability and the pandemic-related struggles of street vendors to the realities of drugs in the surrounding community. Each film was a testament to and celebration of what can happen when like-minded and dedicated educators in the face of disparate and seemingly overwhelming challenges come together to provide cross-classroom interdisciplinary learning experiences.[1]

After the film expo, our team was not the only one impressed by what we had accomplished. EVC, our essential filmmaking partner, had also noticed the high quality of the entirely student-produced films, sharing with Anthony that they were committed to finding funding to continue our collaboration. That is why in the spring of 2022, with our seniors' restlessness signaling that another school year was beginning to close, Anthony and I continued our collaboration. Our mission this time? Fully rekindle the filmmaking flame that was extinguished two years earlier.

Collaborating once again as a science and English duo (in partnership with our special education co-teachers), we set out to help students make another series of environmental justice–focused documentary films. Returning to the initial interdisciplinary approach we had employed pre-pandemic—assigning an environmental justice PSA project in science and the "Who is responsible for protecting my environment?" synthesis essay in English—we deepened our students' background knowledge once more.

Foundational knowledge laid, we then looped EVC and its filmmaking educators into the fold. Working over multiple class periods each day, students captured footage and learned the skills necessary to make a film. As in previous years, each student filmmaking group chose to turn their camera lens upon broad topics. However, this time, thanks to a total return to in-person classes, the lessons students learned were more robust.

When implementing a film project in the classroom, teaching students how to be storytellers is a must. That is why we utilized a "problem, impact, take action" planning framework, which taps into the tenets of critical media pedagogy (learning that is active, authentic, participatory, and empowering) and the idea that marginalized students can become storytellers of inequality through self-produced media.[2] This film planning approach was enacted via storyboarding lessons that helped ensure that each film had a focused vision, logical line of inquiry and guiding question, appropriate story arc, and initial shot list. When the storyboards were complete, students and their films had a path and a direction to making the environmental injustices they witnessed and their solutions come to life.

Using a teaching structure that blurred the lines between science and English and featured two filmmaking class periods per day, students learned a skill in their first class with either Anthony or me in the first period, and then practiced perfecting it in the second period with one of us later in the day. In concrete terms, this may have taken the form of students learning how to conduct an interview properly in their morning filmmaking "science class" and practicing the techniques they had learned by interviewing each other later in the day during "English." Or, perhaps, students learned in the first period with Anthony about how a camera angle from below could be used to uplift and project hero status upon a subject, before applying this technique to their respective films in their second period with me. Regardless of the skill or technique taught and then applied, this coordinated plan allowed students to gradually develop the skills and confidence necessary to make movies that would tell a powerful story and encourage their viewers to take action against injustice.

In addition to gaining filmmaking skills, students needed to gather enough evidence to support the message they hoped to impart to their film's audience. This evidence collection is particularly important for documentary films, which differ from traditional movies owing to their reliance on and grounding in reality.

Students collected real-world evidence through two main approaches. First, they used background and ongoing research to gather relevant statistics, quotes, archival news footage, and other facts that would eventually be interspersed throughout their films. Second, each group was required to bring their film to life via interviews. Indeed, what documentary film doesn't have a few good talking heads?

Interviews could take the form of speaking with subject matter experts, documenting firsthand experiences of community residents, or relaying the perspectives of students' peers and family members. In one particularly memorable interview, students asked a climate change expert how environmental justice communities like theirs could better prepare for an increasingly warm world. In another, students spoke with a group member's mother about her challenges preparing healthy and affordable foods for their family, highlighting the need for food justice. Interview after interview, students revealed their proficiency in filmmaking and ability to tell an evidence-based story.

Our teaching team developed and provided various other supports for our students. The first we utilized was the exemplar. Exemplars, or high-quality work samples from previous years' films, could be used in part or as a whole. Perhaps a still-in-progress film from the current year used establishing shots particularly well or sequenced its storytelling in a logical manner. Maybe another finished film could help inform students how a logical line of inquiry helped enhance a film's final message. The point is that regardless of how much an exemplar is used, it can inform, inspire, and demonstrate to students what is expected and possible.

The second essential support, the critique lesson, was drawn from a mainstay of Anthony's English practice and was particularly useful for providing students feedback on their filmmaking prowess and progress. During each critique, student groups were asked to show video footage demonstrating a particular filmmaking skill or evidence of a required piece of content. After viewing the clip, the entire class—using our project rubric as a guide—would provide verbal and written feedback for the group whose film was under scrutiny. Upon the completion of each critique, groups whose work had been reviewed would have concrete next steps on improving both their craft and quality of work. In this manner, the critique lesson, used in tandem with the exemplar, allowed students to visually see and objectively assess what they have done well and what might still need improvement.

The last step in the filmmaking process was editing. After many hours had been spent collecting footage and gathering supplementary evidence, each film had to be cut and combined into a film piece about five minutes long. Leaning on our classroom partner EVC and its filmmaking professionals, our students were taught how to cut, splice, transition, add audio, adjust levels, and insert subtitles, turning their disparate video and audio clips plus myriad supporting facts into a cohesive documentary film. Eventually, students mastered the art and science of editing, gaining support and receiving crucial, rubric-based feedback via screening their film's rough cuts. After many iterations and increasingly refined adjustments, the environmental justice documentary films were completed.

As in years past, we celebrated. This time, however, our school community was back together in person after a two-year pandemic-imposed interruption. On EJ Expo night (which I sadly missed due to contracting COVID), students and guests gathered in our school's auditorium. They settled into their seats, the decades-old wood-backed chairs creaking in protest yet ultimately holding their occupants firm. Lights were dimmed. An LED projector's bulb slowly warmed, bringing student films and months of hard work into view. Someone pressed play on a nearby laptop. As the films were screened, their mission of documenting environmental injustice and informing those in attendance what they could do to address it came to light, putting on full display the power of a cross-classroom interdisciplinary approach.

The stories I shared in this chapter illustrate why cross-classroom interdisciplinary partnerships are worth pursuing despite their inherent challenges. Indeed, when curricula intertwine, isolated islands become bridged archipelagos, making previously unattainable pedagogical pursuits possible. They are possible because a bridge can connect content knowledge and skills between disparate topics. Because a bridge can save time, allowing students to work across multiple class periods and content areas. Because a bridge can facilitate the transport of materials, spurring the creation of more rigorous projects and higher-quality work products. Because a bridge can unite once disparate communities, helping colleagues construct relationships and learn from one another. And while building a bridge across a chain of islands can be costly—requiring additional time to plan and healthy doses of patience, flexibility, and compromise—once constructed, a bridge has the potential to create a true community of interconnected and interdependent learning environments.

CHAPTER 12

Celebrate Your Success

An Antidote for Burnout and Demoralization

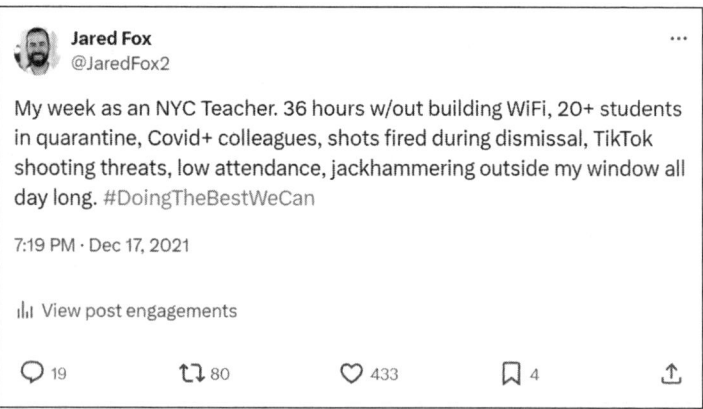

The post above represents the nadir of my time in the classroom. The pandemic was raging, and I was confronted with the most challenging circumstances of my career: a lack of resources, chronically absent students, violence, and a stressful and noisy work environment. All of it was taking its toll. In what, looking back, I would describe as a public venting of my frustrations—not a typical move by me, as I was more a passive observer than an active participant on Twitter (now X)—I turned to the platform's public square. The response to my post surprised me. It was clear that my words had struck a chord and resonated with many.

Teachers who commented on my post shared similar stories of less-than-ideal conditions and classroom influences beyond their control. Other commenters offered genuine support ("Good luck!") and sympathy ("I'm so sorry... This system is beyond broken"). Still others replied with sarcasm: "Living the dream." Looking back on these reactions, I see educators overwhelmed and frustrated and a public disillusioned with how the social circumstances at that time were infiltrating and influencing the classroom experience for teachers and students alike.

An education reporter viewing this post might have a slightly different take, using my words as another example of how teachers are burned out. This oft-identified phenomenon, frequently the reason cited for why teachers leave the profession, is something that I, too, may have been wondering and feeling. A few weeks later, however, I understood that what I was experiencing was not burnout, though that is undoubtedly a common experience for many teachers.

The lack of agency and the general feeling that I could not teach my students in the way I envisioned spoke to something else. The conditions, admittedly unique given the nature of the pandemic, but nonetheless simmering beneath the surface even on the best days in schools, were abrasively rubbing against my moral center. This reality for me and many of my colleagues on the ground and in the field was stirring a response much more profound than burnout. Indeed, it was possible, perhaps even likely, that we were not burned out but demoralized.

Teacher Burnout vs. Demoralization

A few weeks after I posted on X, I attended a teacher workshop hosted by Math for America, the teacher-championing organization referenced earlier in this book that brings math and science teachers together in the pursuit of building community, deepening content knowledge, and improving pedagogical practices. The session's facilitator detailed the work of education researcher Doris Santoro, highlighting her distinction between teacher burnout and the concept of demoralization.

Not long after attending the workshop—and intrigued by what I had learned of Santoro's research and her book, *Demoralized: Why Teachers Leave the Profession They Love and How They Can Stay*—I posted on X again.[1] This time, my message was intended to be educational and uplifting. I wanted to inform the public that what I and my colleagues were experiencing in the classroom was worthy of further examination. Given social media's tendency to promote the sensational, my post, perhaps not surprisingly, garnered significantly less attention.

Jared Fox @JaredFox2 · Jan 20, 2022   •••
To my @UFT @NYCSchools @MathforAmerica colleagues. The last few weeks have been rough. Maybe you're "burned out" and/or demoralized? Did you realize there's a distinction? 'Demoralized' by @DorisASantoro provides a clear distinction and path for renewal.

♡ 1   ↻   ♡ 6   ılıl   🔖 ⬆️

Jared Fox @JaredFox2 · Jan 20, 2022   •••
"Burnout…[assumes] something is wrong w the individual teacher that prevents them from succeeding… In demoralization… educators understand they are facing a conflict btwn their vision of good work and their teaching context"

♡   ↻   ♡ 5   ılıl   🔖 ⬆️

Regardless of who saw this second post, it is apparent now that I was on a more positive path forward and intent on sharing with the world what I was learning and thinking about.

In my post, I also see glimmers of hope stemming from Santoro's distinction between burnout and demoralization. Whereas "burnout" implies that the teacher is flawed and incapable of being successful because of some inherent quality, "demoralization" removes the burden of guilt that educators often feel when much of what is happening inside the classroom is outside their locus of control.[2] This does not absolve teachers from being held accountable for what happens inside their classroom's walls. Instead, it recognizes that the outside and outsized pressures on a teacher, exacerbated by poverty, the degradation of the environment, and, at the time of my post, the ongoing pandemic, are in direct conflict with their moral center.

A Path for Renewal

Realizing and acknowledging the distinction between burnout and demoralization was surprisingly helpful for me as I confronted and coped with the challenges I was facing in the classroom. However, I also wanted to explore more deeply what a "path for renewal," or what Santoro frequently refers to in her book as "re-moralizing," might look like for my teaching. Thankfully, Santoro's work was concerned with more than simply making distinctions and offered approaches to becoming "re-moralized."

In Santoro's book, I found practical solutions for how educators can recharge and renew—ideas on how I could feel seen and have control over my educational sphere of influence. A significant lesson I learned—or, more accurately, was reminded of—is that tapping into a network of like-minded educators can be revitalizing. I was refamiliarized with the idea that being part of a professional learning community like Math for America and working with colleagues like Anthony in an interdisciplinary fashion was something I was already benefiting from but perhaps not leveraging to capacity.

Embracing and enacting the best practices from Santoro's work, I began to reconnect with a wider swath of my colleagues, checking in on how they were doing. In these conversations, we, yes, vented our frustrations but also drew strength and inspiration from our shared practices and commitment to our students. These conversations and connections led to another realization—that there was much we and our students should celebrate. Indeed, honoring our successes as educators, a practice that aligns well with Santoro's strategies for remoralization, is worth pursuing and documenting in detail.[3]

Celebrate Your Success

Too often, educators are left out of the spotlight, never fully recognized for the incredible work they do each day. Sure, there is Teacher

Appreciation Week and the occasional thank-you gift from a parent or student. Yes, sometimes former students may return for a visit to reconnect, grateful for the lessons and guidance their teacher provided years ago. For the most part, however, gratitude for educators flies well below the radar. Most are comfortable and expect this as part of the job. Few educators (perhaps none) enter the profession in pursuit of recognition. However, I argue that individual teachers, students, and society must be more active in sharing their accomplishments.

Acknowledging the risk that this will be construed as being boastful (but still comfortable with that possibility), I want to dedicate the remainder of this chapter to sharing stories and examples of how my colleagues, our students, and I were recognized for our accomplishments. My hope for sharing these tales is twofold. First, I want to demonstrate how tapping into a network of like-minded educators and building a community focused on student success (especially regarding improving the environment) can help resolve feelings of demoralization. Second, I want to inspire and encourage other educators to actively seek out and pursue opportunities for recognition for themselves, their colleagues, and their students. This nearly impossible, often messy, and incredibly beautiful work that teachers do in partnership with their colleagues for the betterment of their students should be acknowledged, shared, and celebrated with the world. Indeed, doing so will uplift those we celebrate and elevate the entire profession along the way.

Celebrate Yourself

A few months before the end of 2019, I received an email from the Fund for the City of New York informing me that I had been nominated for the Sloan Award for Teaching Excellence in Science and Mathematics. Shortly thereafter, I was interviewed, and a few days later, along with a few other of my esteemed math and science teacher colleagues from across the city, I was recognized with the award.

Receiving an award as a teacher is a strange feeling. First and foremost, it is humbling to be acknowledged when dozens, if not hundreds, of other teachers do just as (if not more) impressive things in their classrooms. Second, it is entirely unexpected. Most educators do not get into the teaching game to chase trophies. Instead, we seek to serve and uplift the next generation so they, not us, can go out and win the awards we wholeheartedly believe their creativity and brilliance deserve. That said, being recognized for the work one does in the classroom, as I next recount in the series of events that unfolded a few weeks after receiving the initial email from the Fund for the City of New York, can be amazing.

It's the night of the award ceremony, and I sit on stage with a half-dozen other recipients, perched above an assembled audience that includes my colleagues, students, and family members who bounced downtown from our school aboard a yellow school bus. Midway through the ceremony, it is my turn to be recognized, and, like all the award winners before me, a short, biopic-like film introduces me.[4]

The camera pans across the front of my classroom, zooming through one of the many potted plants perched along its perimeter. It then cuts to the block outside the school to two students bundled in puffy black jackets, hoods pulled over their heads. One, holding a trowel, is pouring flower bulbs from a yellow mesh bag into the other's open hands, a broad smile stretching across the recipient's face.

The camera cuts back to the classroom, where I'm seated in the back corner of the room in front of the windows. Sunshine filters through, landing on plants and the lab sink-turned-makeshift turtle habitat in the background. I wax poetic about science, its purpose being the search for truth, and my attempt to engage students by exploring the environment outside the classroom.

The video continues with street scenes of students digging holes and planting bulbs. An interview with my assistant principal details our school's expeditionary "learning by doing" approach. The Restoring Highbridge intensive is noted, grants won are shared, and the Clean Air Green Corridor project is highlighted.

More audio. I detail the pedagogical intent of connecting what my students are learning in the classroom to the environment around us. Video clips cut from classroom scenes, to still images of students collecting data outside, to their work with the classroom partners highlighted in this book.

The film nears its end. Clips of student projects and audio of me detailing their creativity, imagination, and brilliance fade to black as I work elbow to elbow with a student at my desk.

Back on stage, the film now over, I rise from my seat and approach the podium at the center of the stage. I shake hands with the award representatives from the Fund for the City of New York and the Sloan Foundation. They place an envelope in my hand and return to their seats. Now alone at the podium, I speak directly to my friends, family, colleagues, and students who made the trip. Indeed, how often does one get the opportunity to acknowledge those around them that are so essential to their success? I speak about our collective work together. I thank my family and friends for their unending support. I recognize my colleagues for their partnership. And I tip my cap to my students for their enthusiasm. The assembled audience applauds in approval.

As much as it was nice to be acknowledged, it was equally enjoyable—if not more so—to have the opportunity to share the entire experience with those who made my moment of recognition possible. And while viewing a video highlight reel of my classroom and celebrating my success with those assembled seemed like the ultimate acknowledgement, the good times would soon reach new heights.

When Celebrated, Amplify Your Message

Sitting at my desk a few days after receiving the Sloan Award, doing my best to make it through the last few days that are the whirlwind of emotions before winter break, I opened an enticing email from the Times Square Alliance. Each year, the Alliance, a nonprofit responsible for hosting the annual New Year's Eve party in Times Square, chooses an inspirational theme relevant to the memorable moments of that particular year. In years past, individuals like Muhammad Ali and Supreme Court justice Sonia Sotomayor have served as inspiration, as have entire professions, including journalists and frontline healthcare workers.

In 2019, young climate change crusaders like Greta Thunberg and the Sunrise Movement dominated the news. My students had also been swept up in the groundswell that was (and still is) Fridays for Future climate strikes, inspired one fall afternoon to skip school like Greta and her classmates and attend the massive climate march in Lower Manhattan.

The Times Square Alliance, too, had taken note of this youth-led environmental movement and was interested in acknowledging as much, although with a slightly different twist. As the nonprofit noted in the email I received, it wanted to recognize and honor the New York City teachers of young climate activists by inviting them to push the button that drops the Waterford Crystal ball in the center of Times Square on New Year's Eve.

After reading the email multiple times, I finally realized what had happened. Somehow, I was being tapped to participate in one of the most lavish celebrations on earth. What were the chances? How serendipitous. What an opportunity! And while the irony of being acknowledged for climate and environmental work in the center of Times Square was not lost on me (although I was informed that the square's brightly lit billboards are all LED), I immediately saw this invitation as an opportunity to uplift and celebrate the environmental issues my students and I were working on.

Continuing to come to terms with what I was being asked to do, I reread the invitation again and realized that there was one nota-ble omission—no mention of student participation. Given the role young people played in climate mobilization efforts that year, I felt it was essential that they also be acknowledged and provided with a well-deserved moment under the lights of Times Square. Quickly typing a reply, I conveyed as much to the Alliance, and after a short conversation, they agreed that students should be recognized.

After receiving word that students would have space on the Times Square stage, I accepted the invitation and set out to find two students to join me on the night of the festivities. Determining who should join me was easy—my mind immediately turned to the small group of students who had participated in the Restoring Highbridge intensive that birthed the Clean Air Green Corridor.

After determining which students were interested and available for the event, our collective was caught up in a whirlwind of attention. Before long, myriad news outlets across the United States broadcast our faces and voices. Being cognizant that this could be the extent of my fifteen minutes of fame, I amplified the climate change message that my students and countless young people worldwide had drawn attention to the entire year. I made a conscious effort to call for climate justice during each interview we participated in. I highlighted the local environmental stewardship work my students had been engaged in and their dream for a Clean Air Green Corridor on the block outside our school.

On New Year's Eve, with midnight just a few short hours away, my two students, friends, family members, and I were given all-access passes to the controlled chaos of New Year's Eve in Times Square. Throngs of police and revelers on either side of us, we were ushered past metal barriers and escorted to a pre-event party. Our passes dangling from our necks, we took pictures, filled our bellies with food and age-appropriate drinks, and pinched ourselves throughout the opening moments of our surreal New Year's Eve experience.

Thirty minutes before midnight, appetites sated, and our senses thoroughly indulged, we moved closer to the center of Times Square. While gathered in a small reception tent, sheltered from the creeping cold and massive crowd, we received word of an interview request from our local news station. Soon after that, we climbed high above Times Square into the massive bleacher-like scaffolding of the media riser. Peering across a sea of people and positioned shoulder to shoulder, with Times Square's flashing billboards illuminating either side of us, we shared our message for climate action.

As the reporter turned the microphone to my students—the same students who only a few months earlier had questioned whether anyone cared about the environmental injustices facing their community—they shared how much it meant for them to be able to broadcast to the world what they had been doing. Calling for a more just and sustainable future, they invited all who were watching to join them in their efforts. Astutely catching the look of pride on my face, the reporter turned the microphone to me and allowed me to acknowledge and recognize my students' efforts.

Ten minutes before midnight, we were escorted to the top of a long staircase. Upon cresting the final step, we encountered a brightly lit and ostentatiously decorated stage. As we took in the spotlighted scene, we were greeted by the evening's broadcasting director. Before long, we received frantic instructions on where to stand and how to press the button to drop the ball and ring in the new year.

We took our positions with mere minutes to go before the start of 2020, the beginning of a new decade that we hoped would foster a renewed commitment and embrace of climate change activism—before it was dramatically altered by other, more pressing matters of social justice like the inequities wrought by COVID-19 and murder of George Floyd. My students and I, along with another Sloan Award winner and her students, were arranged on either side of New York City mayor Bill de Blasio and his wife, Chirlane McCray. We anxiously awaited our moment. Seconds remained. Then, as instructed, we each placed one hand on a purple glowing orb—a miniature replica of the giant Waterford Crystal ball perched high above Times Square. The last chords of John Lennon's "Imagine" were played.

All eyes and a sea of camera lenses focused their attention on us. Collectively, we pressed the button.

Slowly.

Steadily.

The Waterford Crystal ball made its descent and we turned to watch.

The final sixty seconds of 2019 upon us.

Ten seconds now. I raised my fist in the air to signal solidarity with the young people worldwide who believed that environmental activism and their planet were causes worthy of our full attention.

"3, 2, 1... Happy New Year!"

Fireworks burst into the air; confetti rained down upon us. I turned and saluted each of my students for all that they had done and would surely soon accomplish. We lingered on stage as the revelers around us embraced. We danced to Frank Sinatra's "New York, New York." We soaked up every drop of the celebratory air, but, like all good things, our night and our moment had ended.

Returning to our school building—a new year realized—we were greeted as celebrities. Instead of basking in our glory, however, we got to work. Wanting to keep the momentum we had garnered from our elevated platform alive, my students, with support from Futures Ignite and me, penned an op-ed that was featured in a pair of local media publications. Reflecting on their New Year's Eve moment, our Clean Air Green Corridor environmental justice warriors wrote, "When we stood on stage we were both nervous and proud." They also highlighted their ongoing work to beautify the neighborhood— "we have already redesigned our school gardens and beautified our block"—and closed their piece with a call to action and renewed commitment to activism: "We crave the opportunity to play an active role in climate solutions and be a part of the youth-led climate movement."[5]

Seeing my students' op-ed in print was inspirational. This public recognition of their work made me feel that what I was doing in the classroom mattered, spotlighting one of the main reasons I had entered the teaching profession—to provide young people with the opportunity to pursue pathways for environmental improvement in their local community.

The last few weeks of 2019 and the first few of 2020 seemed like the pinnacle of my time in the classroom. New Year's Eve. Center of Times Square. Crystal ball. Fireworks. Confetti. These moments represented the highest of highs. An amalgamation of events more often reserved for political victors on election night or NFL players after Super Bowl victories, not the work of a teacher and their students. Recognizing this reality, I did my best to soak it all in, seeing my serendipitous circumstance as the accumulation and culmination of all the hours spent planning, organizing, grading, collaborating, and seeking to uplift the brilliance of my students. I celebrated these moments intentionally, because I knew they would be ephemeral and that the nature of the profoundly complex work of being an educator would not allow me to rest on my laurels. It was inevitable that I would return from orbit. It was all but assured that I would regress to the mean. However, I did not expect the world to be entirely turned on its head.

Celebrate Your Colleagues

I don't mean to dwell on the impact that the COVID-19 pandemic had on educational spaces. Still, I must mention it again to emphasize just how challenging the early (and ongoing) days of the pandemic were for educators and their students. The difference between where I was on the day schools closed in mid-March of 2020 and where I was just a few weeks earlier, at the dawn of a new decade in the center of Times Square, was stark. All the momentum that my students and I had garnered to inform and encourage others to better the environment around them seemed to come to a screeching halt. Overnight, our work had gone from beautifying the blocks around our school to teaching and learning within the black-boxed void that was virtual learning.

I share this juxtaposition to highlight two things. First, it explains why midway through 2021—when the pandemic was still in full swing—I shared the post on X that I discussed at the opening of this chapter. Second, it helps me remember how being recognized and celebrated for my success inspired me to uplift my colleagues. And, as it happens, not long after these commemorations, my colleague and interdisciplinary collaborator Anthony Voulgarides approached me with a request.

Every year, EL Education, the umbrella organization coordinating a national school network that embraces an expeditionary learning approach, recognizes a teacher of the year. Anthony, a one-time finalist for the award himself, was interested in nominating our colleague, Erick Espin. He asked me to supplement the written application he was composing by creating a short video of student testimonials.

Knowing firsthand how powerful and uplifting a video compilation of one's teaching practices can be, I enthusiastically embraced Anthony's ask. Soon after, I found myself sitting at my dining room table, viewing video clips and listening intently to the words of Erick's former students. Hearing what Erick's students had said about him was inspirational. Student after student spoke of the "energy" in Erick's classroom. How he was a "special teacher" and "made [his students] feel smart." They spoke of his ability to inspire—"he wants you to be someone"—and how their shared cultural background made them feel like "he is us." Collectively, the clips spoke to the creativity of Erick's teaching practices, his ability to build relationships, and the connections he helped his students see between the history he taught and the current circumstances of today.

With the application deadline for the award quickly approaching, I cobbled together a highlight reel of Erick's former students, and, together with Anthony's narrative, we submitted the nomination. A few days later, uncertain if Erick would win but wanting to celebrate his success, we shared what we had created. Erick was humbled and grateful to be acknowledged. Our nomination team, which also included a number of other colleagues, felt good about recognizing his efforts. Publicly celebrating Erick's success was a win-win.

Given the powerful experience I had crafting and sharing the application with Erick, I highly recommend that all educators participate in this practice. Celebrations of our colleagues can be simple. They can take the form of conversations in which we let them know that we see, hear, and appreciate them, or they become actionable and essential ingredients of meeting agendas. Acknowledgment can be a quick email, text, or handwritten note. Regardless of their frequency or what form they take, such actions can help build community and push against the insidious creep of teacher burnout and demoralization. However, if you do decide to submit a nomination for teacher of the year for one of your colleagues, be warned that they, like Erick, might just be acknowledged as its winner.

Celebrate the Future

One of the accepted downsides to being a teacher is that you may never really know what impact you are having on the lives of your students. As I have shared, a former student might return for an uplifting visit that can inspire action. For the most part, however, these encounters are rare, brief, and short-lived. As a result, most educators (as my friend and former teacher Chris Emdin astutely notes in the foreword of this book) do not see the long-term fruits of their efforts.

Yes, we may hear through the grapevine about a former student's accomplishments—they have graduated from college, started a family, or earned a career promotion—but for the most part, the paths our students have taken are hidden from view. In truth, this is okay, for we as teachers accept that our students have moved on and we also have our hands full with the next group of students filling our classroom. At the same time, however, it is possible for long-term connections and relationships that initially started at school to be renewed and sustained.

Just before a pending move would take me away from New York City and the classroom spaces I had loved and inhabited for nearly two decades, I serendipitously reconnected with a former student-turned-environmental science teacher, Sabrina Diaz (now Sabrina Mujica). Sabrina was a quiet but focused, determined, and capable twelfth grader in my science classroom. She also continuously engaged in our classroom lessons and created beautiful final projects showcasing her content understanding and passion for the environment.

When we reconnected, Sabrina shared that what she had learned and done in my classroom more than a decade ago had inspired her to pursue a career in environmental education. Now, she wanted to bring that same passion and desire for environmental justice she harbored as a student to the young people she taught at a school in the neighborhood where she was born.

I was blown away. Here I was, Sabrina's former teacher, struggling to grasp what it would mean when I stepped away from the classroom, finding solace in knowing that someone as dedicated and talented as herself was committed to cultivating a learning environment in her classroom similar to the one she experienced in mine. I was inspired and offered Sabrina my support. She graciously accepted.

Over the summer, we met multiple times—me settling into a new city, and Sabrina embracing the challenges and hopes of a new school year. Together, a teacher and their former student collaborated as colleagues. We brainstormed curricular ideas. We troubleshot logistical issues. Sabrina decided to introduce the Environmental Justice Expo project into her classroom.

Throughout the school year, as Sabrina's ideas developed for what the expo would look like for her students and in her school, we continued to connect. I offered Sabrina resources, materials, and advice. In return, she provided me hope and inspiration in the form of young people's unbridled enthusiasm and creativity in the name of environmental action and justice.

That spring, Sabrina invited me to her classroom. Her students were hosting their very own expo. They had done the research. They had documented the environmental injustices in their community. They were ready to present and share what they had learned in partnership and celebration with an outside audience of experts. Environmental justice champion and MacArthur "genius" fellow Majora Carter would be there. I had to be there too.

I entered Sabrina's school nervous and as a relative stranger but felt immediately at home upon stepping into her classroom. Around me, I saw anxious students waiting beside beautifully curated projects highlighting inequities in air quality, green space, and other local environmental injustices. To launch the expo, Sabrina welcomed all who had gathered, graciously noting the presence of her former teacher, before providing context for her class's work and their pursuit of bettering the world around them. Then, like any great teacher, she turned the classroom over to her students, who displayed the full power of crafting a learning environment both within and outside a classroom's walls.

On the train ride home from New York, I took a moment to revel in Sabrina's success and acknowledge the bittersweet feeling I was experiencing after leaving my classroom behind. In some ways, I longed to be in Sabrina's position. Building relationships with students and working alongside like-minded colleagues. Making my vision of a dynamic learning environment come to life. As I reflected, I also felt a deep sense of gratitude for the opportunity to be a part of Sabrina's students' expo because, in truth, despite my recent departure from the halls of my former school, I continued to wrestle with the reverberations of having confronted, overcome, and continually beaten back the insidious creep of the educational landscape's ability to demoralize.

Fast-forward to today. It is late 2024. As I write the final few lines of this book, sharing much of what I have learned, experienced, and believe about how to be an effective teacher, I am hopeful that my call to action for educators (and society writ large) to unabashedly celebrate successes will have resonated with you. I am also optimistic that the stories I have shared and the actions and approaches I have detailed herein will inspire others (perhaps even you) to pursue the creation of a meaningful learning environment full of passion and joy. Indeed, as I sit here today, another new school year is underway, and an ordinarily magical time that should be reserved for renewal and the building of relationships has already been marred by another deadly shooting and continued reports of the myriad challenges facing a system that can feel irreparable. However, having immersed myself in creating meaningful learning environments for hundreds of students over the past two decades, I refuse to succumb to the pull of demoralization and instead insist that I—that we—use the proof of past experiences as evidence that a brighter future awaits.

I am hopeful because I have seen what happens when students examine the history of their local environment, collect data as scientists in pursuit of advocating for a cause, and explore ecosystems across the street, throughout their city, and further afield. I have seen what happens when classrooms partner with each other and experts, creating unimaginable synergistic solutions to authentic problems. I have seen what can occur when students are met where they are and provided with structures and routines that support acquiring knowledge and skills, resulting in a newfound confidence in their ability to learn. I am hopeful because of my colleagues. Because of the burgeoning career of new teachers like Sabrina, who similarly believe in the power and ability of educators to craft learning environments capable of transforming student lives and the world.

After the Classroom

A few years removed from my nearly two decades in the classroom, and blessed with the good fortune of having spent over half of this time in a philosophically aligned and teacher's soul–nourishing expeditionary learning setting, I am cognizant of how easy it is to lose sight of the challenges a teacher faces in their day-to-day life. Indeed, the work of a teacher is perhaps one of the most difficult jobs in the world to master. Not only are educators dealing with the uniqueness of dozens of individual minds, each with their own distinct schema, perspectives, lived experience, possible trauma, and preferences, but they are doing so in a system that is severely damaged if not entirely broken. This is not to discount the incredible work happening within individual classrooms, schools, districts, and some state offices but to draw attention to the fact that our education system is in crisis. Chronic absenteeism, gun and other forms of violence, teacher attrition and vacancies, high-stakes testing, increased privatization, underfunding, crumbling building infrastructure, student behavior and mental health concerns, and continued segregation by race and income (particularly in urban areas) are forcing educators to teach—and here I quote from author and former teacher Sandra Cisneros's *A House of My Own: Stories from My Life*—"because the world we live in is a house on fire and the people we love are burning."[1]

Admirable? Of course. Heroic? For sure. Ideal? Certainly not.

And because teachers—because I—had to operate within a system that was and still is inadequate for the teaching of the whole child—mind, body, and soul—I must also recognize that the actions, approaches, and stories I shared in this book did not detail the many and multiple failed attempts of other, less impactful, parts of my pedagogy. However, while I am betting on the assumption that reading stories about my success was more enjoyable for you than it would have been reading about my failures, I must admit that even the actions and approaches I deemed successful enough to share herein were not without their flaws. In these moments of struggle where, despite my best efforts, I still failed to engage all students in the learning process, I, yes, worked tirelessly toward my idealized learning environment goals, but also balanced these lofty pursuits with a focus on the immediate needs of the young people in my classroom. This necessary back-and-forth between the ideal and the real will always make teaching simultaneously messy and beautiful.

Despite the failures I'm admitting to here, I hope educators (perhaps you) will use this book and the actions and approaches I shared as inspirational impetus to put students' voices, lived experiences, and surrounding environment at the center of their work. Indeed, young people yearn for opportunities to be seen and become leaders both in and outside the classroom. They desire to join the movement calling for a more just and sustainable world. They welcome, even demand, these opportunities to engage in this work because they, like their teachers, know that their world and futures are on fire and they are the ones who will be most badly burned by the failure to act.

I hope that in using the actions, approaches, and anecdotes in this book, you craft a similarly meaningful learning environment for the students in your classroom. I hope you find the courage and confidence to teach your passions and pursue pathways for your professional development. I hope your classroom will work with experts in and out of the school building to synergize your collective impact and effect change. I hope you ask your students to engage in localized learning experiences and collect data as scientists, historians, mathematicians, and experts of any other profession represented by the content and skills you teach to prepare them for college and career success. I hope you will celebrate the success of your past, present, and future students, as well as the accomplishments of you and your colleagues. I hope these same actions and approaches that connected my classroom's environment to the real world make learning more engaging and meaningful for your students and you, their teacher.

And while I am confident that educators will, as they always have, continue to show up and advocate for the best interests and brilliance of the young people under their care, I am less confident that we as a society will show up for educators. Because, if we want teachers to pursue the creation of impactful and meaningful learning environments for their students (and themselves), we must move beyond hope and commit to sustained and focused action.

If we want our students and teachers to be successful, if we want our country to continue to be a world leader and innovator, if we want to heal our society's deep divisions and open wounds, then we must do better—much better—for our schools.

We cannot just admire teachers from afar—paying them lip service for their selfless work; instead, we must act and reward them with status—signified by higher pay, a professionalized work environment, beautiful school buildings and classrooms, and true representation at the table when education-related policy decisions are made. And yes, we must not forget about the students, because as many will rightly suggest, centering their needs is paramount to ensuring the recovery of a system in crisis and the success of our shared future. However, if we are serious about healing our education system, then we also must acknowledge, uplift, and reproduce learning environments that are as supportive of teachers as they are to the students under their care.

Actions and Approaches for Connecting Classrooms to the Real World

To read about how *Learning Environment* was created, visit https://jaredfox.substack.com.

Visit www.jaredfox.education for help and resources that bring the actions and approaches highlighted in this book to life in your educational setting.

For a quick reference guide and additional details about the actions and approaches in this book, see below.

Implementing a Localized Learning Approach (Chapter 1)

Localized learning requires physically accessing the surrounding community's resources (parks, organizations, museums, shorelines, even the sidewalk—the closer to your school, the better). Localized learning should entail venturing outside the school building for at least a class period and, more often, an entire day. You can plan and carry out trip experiences independently, but they will be made more powerful (and logistically less challenging) when you recruit partners to help facilitate with and alongside you.

Before Leaving the Classroom

- Write grants. Ideally, all localized learning experiences and student trips will be adequately funded. When they are not, consider applying for funding opportunities and awards to equip your classroom with scientific tools and adventures. Don't be daunted. Remember, grant money is intended to be given away, and there are many individuals ready to help crowdfund your latest and greatest ideas, with education-centric DonorsChoose. org being a great place to start.

- Provide students with the *content, context, and skills* they will need (and benefit from) during a localized learning experience. Doing so helps familiarize students with what they are learning and being asked to do and, as a result, allows you to be more available to fully support them.

- *Content*: This refers to the background knowledge students need before leaving the classroom to better understand what they will see, learn, and do.

- *Context*: Providing contextual answers to "why" questions—e.g., "Why are we going to the park across the street from the school?"—helps students better understand how an activity fits into the larger scope of learning in the classroom.

- *Skills*: Prepare students with the scientific or content-specific practices they will use (e.g., data collection) when they are outside of the school building and may one day utilize in the real world.

Logistics

- Well before any localized learning experience, know where you are going, how you will get there, and what materials you will need. Coordinate and confirm your travel plans with students and families, your school, grade-level team, chaperones, and the site you will visit (ensuring they know how and when you will arrive).

- Trips and fieldwork can be physically demanding with dirty conditions. Proper drinks, snacks, and footwear are essential.

- When possible, walk to your field site. Wheeled transportation to the destination may be faster, but a walk can be a localized learning experience in its own right.

When Outside the Classroom

- When arriving at your field site, consider starting with an opening circle—a physical arrangement in which everyone faces each other. The opening circle can help relay expectations and outline the day's learning plan within the context of a trip's setting. The reading of a poem, quote, or short excerpt can help ground and connect your class to the work and learning that awaits, as well as provide a sense of place.

- Bringing students into natural spaces can be discomforting, especially for students who live in urban areas. Allowing students to vent their frustrations and reminding them of the opportunity that learning in natural spaces can provide may help calm anxieties.

- Focus on joy—yes, leaving the classroom should allow students to learn something new and connect what they are doing in the classroom to the wider world around them, but it should also be a lot of fun. Making trips joyful is essential to crafting successful out-of-school experiences for students.

- Consider having students document their interaction with the world around them in a nature journal. Doing so can be a great way to collect data and observations in the field and has been demonstrated to help students reduce stress, boost mood, and facilitate connections to the environment and each other.[1]

Back in the Classroom

- Whatever students are asked to do during a trip should be, at minimum, reviewed and, at best, incorporated into the overarching context of a unit of study.

- Prepare a digital slideshow and show it the day after an experience in the field. Hang physical photos from the trip around the room. Visual reminders of time spent outside the classroom help facilitate reflective conversations (presenting opportunities to review content learned and add additional context) and remind students of how much fun they had on their trip (a focus on joy).

- Have students write or reflect on their experience. Use a claim-evidence-reasoning framework to analyze and evaluate collected data.

Additional Actions and Approaches

- Extend your time in the field by adopting an "intensive" or after-school approach (chapters 8 and 9). Think creatively about how the regular school day can be structured to extend learning time outside the school building. Incentivize students to continue their work with you in your classroom during after-school enrichment opportunities. Seek out partners to provide additional support or even stipends.

Pursuing Professional Development (Chapter 1)

Not all professional development opportunities are created equal. Let your educational philosophy and teacher compass guide you when pursuing professional learning.

- Look for professional development that is not just a "one-off" experience. Extend your learning over multiple sessions or even consecutive summers to incorporate new practices into your teaching.

- Take advantage of "educator evenings" offered by organizations and institutions. These exclusive events may allow early access to a site, let you assess partnership opportunities, and connect with like-minded educators. When you attend them, take notes. Your notes may help you shape learning activities for your classroom and prepare your students for an eventual visit. And don't forget to follow up with those like-minded educators. Building community requires follow-through.

- Join a community or organization dedicated to uplifting the teaching profession. Connecting to and learning with and from like-minded educators can result in powerful and unique professional development opportunities and experiences.

- Many professional development programs offer stipends, materials for the classroom, or both. Use these offers as incentives and as a means to gain resources for yourself and your classroom.

- Use professional development to become trained or certified (hands-on and in-person experiences are best). Earning a credential can help you access previously inaccessible resources and support and potentially lead to an increase in your salary.

- While not often considered professional development, a cross-classroom interdisciplinary approach (chapter 11) and partnering with colleagues in different content areas can be a compelling professional learning experience. Observing, collaborating with, and teaching alongside your colleagues may help students see the interconnectedness between their classes and improve your pedagogy as well as your understanding of a different content area. Building a community in this way can also be uplifting and revitalizing, pushing back against feelings of demoralization.

Students as (Community) Scientists (Multiple Chapters)

An expeditionary learning-by-doing approach—field trips as fieldwork—can help students act and see themselves as scientific professionals. By making observations and collecting, analyzing, and evaluating data, students can learn new content and skills, become active participants in the scientific community, and gain insight and inspiration on how to advocate for change.

- A claim-evidence-reasoning argumentative writing approach (chapter 1) may help students learn to think critically and provide explanations and rationale for their ideas. Using this approach multiple times over the year (same skill with different content) allows for the provision of actionable feedback to students. This repetition also allows teachers to measure student growth over time.

- A systems thinking approach to curriculum and lesson design can help students understand how separate parts are related to an interconnected whole (e.g., wastewater treatment plant, the human body, ecosystems). A modified jigsaw activity (chapter 5) that asks students to work in groups, become experts on one part of a system, and then teach what they have learned to their classmates is one approach for incorporating systems thinking into the classroom. Other methods include leveraging the local environment—e.g., visiting the inside of a wastewater treatment plant (chapter 5) or visiting a disturbed ecosystem and helping to restore a park (chapter 8).

- When preparing students for a hands-on activity, previewing the procedure remains a best practice. However, to create an intentional feeling of mystery or a sense of friendly competition in the classroom (chapter 5), consider forgoing a procedural preview.

- Publicly accessible scientific reports can be used as "anchor" texts (documents, books, artifacts, or other readings that are referenced and returned to multiple times throughout a course of learning) to develop curriculum and teach data analysis (chapter 6).

- Ask students to use the data within a scientific report to evaluate or critique the conclusions it provides. (Are they accurate, reasonable, and trustworthy?)

- Comparing the report's data and conclusions to known health and safety standards can sharpen your students' critical lens.

- After completing student evaluations and critiques, consider analyzing the raw data (if available) that was gathered for the scientific report.

- When analyzing raw data, explicitly teach students how to use data analysis tools—e.g., spreadsheet applications.

- If raw data analyses reveal a problem or contradict the original report, encourage students to become community scientists and activists by bringing this issue/inaccuracy to the forefront. Provide opportunities for them to present their findings in front of visiting experts or decision-makers, asking those assembled for help resolving any problems uncovered.

- Turn the science data students collect (the immediate environment around your school is a great place to start) into presentations for a local community board or elected official. Evidence-based, image-heavy student presentations (like ArcGIS StoryMaps) are crowd-pleasers and may rally those with access to the levers of power to your side.

- As students become comfortable with the data they collect and the content they have learned, provide opportunities for them to teach their peers (providing feedback and rehearsal time along the way). Host a daylong teach-in where students design lessons and deliver them to their classmates to help spread awareness of what they have learned and encourage others in the school community to get involved via community action projects (chapter 8).

- Dissections, especially those of still-living creatures (be sure to follow proper ethics guidelines), can provide an engaging learning experience for students and teachers (chapter 9). Perform demonstration dissections under stereomicroscopes. Create a shared multimodal microscope learning experience by connecting this magnification tool to a digital camera and visual display for all to see.

- Using field guides is a great way to help students identify the organisms in their surroundings and hone their questioning and observation skills. Digital field guides and nature identification apps can further supplement the learning experience by being paired with those of the paper-bound variety.

- Mobile labs, if available, are a great way to turn your students into practicing scientists. A lab on wheels, which can either meet you in the field or pull up to your school's doorstep, can remove many trip-related logistical headaches and bring myriad other benefits, such as research-grade equipment and a professional staff of science experts, directly to your students.

Shifting the Gaze (Chapter 8)

Shifting the gaze asks students to look at the world around them slightly differently (as scientists may do). It may encourage students to think critically about the world around them, become community scientists, or garner new insights that can inspire environmental action. Conducting a street tree census is one way to shift the gaze from viewing the natural world as an amorphous place disconnected from our day-to-day lives to one full of interdependent and dynamic living and non-living things that we interact with and depend upon.

Conducting a Street Tree Census

- Our efforts must be intentional if we want students to get off their devices and engage with the natural world. That said, sometimes it's also okay to embrace technology—allowing students to use their devices out of the classroom to collect data mimics what many practicing scientists do in the field.

- Not much green space is needed to shift students' gaze—collecting data as a part of an official or unofficial street tree census (chapter 8) is one way to embrace this approach. Partner with your local Parks Department as a part of a tree census to train students on how to measure and evaluate the health of trees near their school.

- No upcoming tree census or Parks Department available? Train them yourself. Field guides (paper or digital), serving as resources for identifying tree species and measuring the diameter of trunks and overall health, are great places to start.

- Compile the data students collect during a street tree census into an annually updated database, allowing each class to track tree growth and health.

- Incorporate the data you collect into StoryMaps or Field Maps (another ArcGIS tool).

- Provide students with the attire, equipment, and tools to look the part and fully participate as scientific professionals. Neon safety vests are all the rage!

- When students are in the field collecting data, allow them (with supervision) to share what they are doing with community members. These informal chats can be a great way for students to reinforce what they are doing and learning by teaching it to others. In addition, community members may also learn something new or even want to join in your efforts and support your cause.

- After conducting a census, plant a tree with students. It will give you all the feels.

The Mystery Piece (Chapters 2 Through 5)

At the beginning of a new learning unit or lesson, it is essential to ignite student curiosity. One way to do this is via the mystery piece. The mystery piece, according to EL Education, "captures students' interest in the topic they are about to begin studying. It piques their curiosity."[2] I used the mystery piece in my classroom to help students activate preexisting schema or background knowledge. The best mystery pieces will utilize thought-provoking material, "hook" students, and encourage them to generate more questions than answers. Once students are hooked, capitalize on their engagement by linking their curiosity to the next logical piece of learning.

Intriguing Images Mystery Piece (Chapter 2)

- While students are participating in an image-focused mystery piece activity, consider using the "See, Think, Wonder" exercise, a visible thinking practice created by the Harvard Graduate School of Education research initiative Project Zero.

- See: Students make observations ("What do you see?")

- Think: Students share ideas on what they perceive happening in the image ("What do you think?")

- Wonder: Students generate new questions based on their observations and thoughts ("What do you wonder or want to know more about?")

Transforming the Physical Classroom Space Mystery Piece (Chapter 4)

- Scatter discarded plastic bottles across the classroom to kick off a unit on the bottled water industry, prepare a fictionalized crime scene for a forensics unit, turn tables and chairs upside as though an earthquake has occurred. Altering the classroom's physical space can help capture students' attention and encourage them to use their imagination to think critically about how a transformed learning environment is related to a unit of study.

The Multiple-Day Mystery Piece (Chapter 5)

- A mystery piece need not be limited to a lesson or unit's opening moments. It can also take place over multiple days. One way to do this is by utilizing experts as a part of the mystery piece experience, or bringing in an artifact from the field for deeper examination.

Socratic Circles (Chapter 2)

At its core, a Socratic circle is a student-led conversation. In addition to the practices I adopted below, see Matt Copeland's book, *Socratic Circles: Fostering Critical and Creative Thinking in Middle and High School*, as an additional resource.

Before a Socratic Circle

- Select a complex but engaging text related to the unit of study.

- Dedicate time for an in-class reading day. Expect students to annotate the text (e.g., writing one-sentence summaries at logical stopping points throughout the text). Support struggling readers by pulling them into a small group but also invite all students to attend (they can help read along with you to those students who may have challenges comprehending the text).

- Provide students with the questions they will be expected to discuss before Socratic circle day. Attach them to the end of the assigned reading. Expect and encourage them to use the provided questions to prepare for the classroom conversation.

- On the day of a Socratic circle, transform the classroom learning space. Create two circles: an inner circle of chairs for the "discussion group" and an outer circle of tables for the "listening/feedback group."

During a Socratic Circle

Students

- One student from the inner circle starts the conversation by selecting a question from the list provided. They answer, and then others share their ideas. Students choose when to transition to a new question.

- The inner circle talks for at least fifteen minutes, then the outer circle provides feedback on what they heard.

Teachers

- Review classroom norms and expectations before beginning a Socratic circle discussion. Emphasize and model respectful dialogue.

- Only interject if the conversation goes too far off course or misinformation is being shared.

- Consider using a discussion rubric as a guardrail and guide to direct student feedback and enhance inner-circle conversation.

- To increase the rigor and quality of discussions, consider scoring conversations for participation and an individual student's ability to use text-based evidence to support and synthesize their ideas. If scoring, take lots of notes—verbatim, if possible. Recording the conversation is another option. Teachers and students alike can later analyze the recordings, identifying moments worthy of praise or in need of improvement.

After a Socratic Circle

- Allow students opportunities to participate in the conversation even after it ends. Encourage students to submit written responses to the provided questions to improve their grades or extend their learning.

- Make Socratic circles an ongoing practice in the classroom. Hosting them over multiple units across the school year can provide opportunities to measure student growth in reading and discussion skills.

Gallery Walk + Jigsaw Activity (Chapter 3)

Gallery walks are learning experiences where students move around the classroom to a series of stations, working independently (and often silently) to take notes and build their background knowledge. Jigsaws ask students to become experts on a particular topic or text and teach their classmates what they have learned. Combining the best components of these two popular activities is an option and can turn students into co-teachers and co-constructors of each other's knowledge.

- Present student pairs with a challenge that will breach the limits of their pre-existing schema (zone of proximal development).

- While students are working their way through the challenge, make careful observations. As they approach frustration or disengage, provide timely scaffolded clues (definitions, examples, new information, video resources, etc.).

- When clues are exhausted, transition to a "gallery walk." One student from each pair stays at their table as an "explainer" of the duo's work while the other travels around the room as a "gatherer" to glean new insights from other "explainers" at different tables.

- After the gallery walk, ask students to return to their original pairs to incorporate newly learned insights into solving the original challenge.

- Debrief as a group. Depending on the next step in the learning unit, answers to the challenge may or may not be revealed. Indeed, sometimes it is better to focus on the learning process over the learning outcome.

Interdisciplinary Ideations (Chapter 11)

An interdisciplinary approach to curriculum and lesson design can be particularly powerful. Providing students with a historical context, working with a teaching partner, and capitalizing on the local environment helped my students see connections between the scientific past and the present day. Using a case study is one possible approach to incorporating history into the classroom.

Case Studies

Shaping curriculum around local case studies such as lead exposure in the drinking water supply (chapter 3), the bottled water industry (chapter 4), combined sewer overflows and harbor health (chapter 6), and nearby disrupted ecosystems (chapter 8) can help students connect present-day issues to the past, and inspire and inform action on and engagement in the environment.

Partnering with Experts (Multiple Chapters)

Expand your definition and understanding of what or who an expert is. Experts can be solo industry insiders, community-based organizations, college students, or neighborhood residents. Because of their varied lived experiences, each can contribute a unique perspective and additional layer to the learning environment in the classroom. A classroom visit by an expert signals to students that what they are learning and doing matters and is relevant to the world around them.

- The thought of trying to build a fully established relationship with an expert or organization can feel daunting. Start small. Send an email. Invite an expert to your class. When they visit, assess how they and their message fit with you, your students, and your curriculum. If all goes well, invite them back for a return visit or create a small-group pilot program to determine whether a larger-scale partnership is prudent. Then, start dreaming of creating synergy between your shared goals and interests. Design curriculum together, host expos, participate in neighborhood beautification efforts—do more working together than you could have ever accomplished alone.

- Before an expert visit, consider providing students with a baseline of background knowledge. A content-based assessment (quiz or test) is one way to lay this foundation and provide students with a contextualized connection to an expert's visit. Also provide information about your class and course to the visiting expert(s). Don't be afraid to provide explicit instructions and set goals and expectations for what you want their visit to accomplish.

- Experts can make magic happen in the classroom. Ask them to demonstrate and perform the work they do in their place of work in front of your class, or ask them to share examples of the products and tools they use to carry out their work (chapters 4 and 6). Then, provide opportunities for your students to use the expert's professional tools and models in the subsequent work they carry out. These real-world interactions and exemplars can increase the rigor of the task at hand and the craftsmanship (professionalism) of finished work products.

- Ask experts to evaluate student work as panelists or judges. The presence of experts in the classroom at student presentations can create a heightened sense of urgency around deadlines and serve as another way to increase the rigor and quality of student work products. Give experts a rubric and ask them to provide actionable feedback. After the evaluation, allow students additional time to incorporate expert comments into their final drafts.

- Community member experts can use their local knowledge and firsthand experiences in the neighborhood to teach your students about ongoing problems and issues. Invite them into the classroom to share or ask them to lead a guided tour of the local environment (chapter 8). Their point of view may shed light on or reaffirm your students' lived experience.

- If working with a partner with a specific skill set or expertise you want students to acquire—e.g., ArcGIS StoryMaps (chapter 10)—consider asking them to create a video tutorial to support student learning. First, deliver a whole-class demonstration, then have students watch the tutorial and build a replica or practice the same skill demonstrated in the tutorial. (This will allow you to focus on supporting skill attainment, not content proficiency.) Finally, ask students to apply their learned skills to a similar but novel assessment. A skill-based tutorial video will allow students to work at their own pace and lets you provide an on-demand learning experience for students who may have missed a lesson or need additional practice. Yes, video production is a heavy lift, but once the tutorials are created, they can be used every year.

- Keep pushing boundaries for what is possible with partnerships. Lean into established relationships to support curriculum design, classroom teaching, and the presentation and celebration of student work. A deeper partnership can bring meaningful learning experiences and opportunities to classrooms and partners alike.

Projects and Presentations (Multiple Chapters, Chapter 4 Focus)

- Share a project's end goal and due date early and often. Create and frequently revisit a student-facing project calendar. Reminding students of deadlines and final events can help them better structure their time each day and foster a sense of urgency in the classroom.

- Consider intentionally broadening the content covered by a project. Allow students to survey a variety of relevant topics related to the overarching project task before specializing and becoming experts on one. For example, when I taught students about environmental justice, there were a variety of specialized topics (open and green space, food justice, air quality, etc.) that they could choose to focus on for their final work product.

- Create a menu of options and project formats for students to demonstrate their understanding and construct their final project. Embrace equitable practices by varying the number of project components that students of different abilities or groups of different sizes must complete.

- Share exemplary final projects from the previous year. It can inspire and inform students about what to aim for in their work.

- Once students select a project topic, consider curating credible sources to deepen their background knowledge. Helping to facilitate the research process this way may minimize misconceptions during this knowledge acquisition phase and make the entire project production period more efficient.

- An early rough draft of an assigned project is a great way to encourage students to move from project ideation to creation.

Setting a deadline only a few days after students have started a project typically does the trick.

- Ask students to share their rough drafts in front of the class (or a small group). This will allow you to better understand who is succeeding and who may need additional support. Students, by seeing each other's work, can be inspired to push their own projects to new heights.

- When students are presenting rough drafts, ask them to critique their peers according to the project's scoring rubric. This will remind students how they will be graded when they complete the project and generate feedback to help them determine their next steps.

- Find opportunities for students to present their work in front of their community (e.g., expert panel or EJ Expo; see below). A public forum is rife with opportunities to make culturally relevant, authentic, and meaningful connections between students' work and the real world. For the students, knowing that they must present in front of a gathered audience increases the rigor of a task, encourages craftsmanship, pushes the quality of finished products to new heights, and can mimic the experiences of the professional workplace. ArcGIS StoryMaps, with their highly visual images and maps from the environment along with their narrative format, can help students craft more engaging presentations.

Hosting Your Own Expo (Chapter 7)

- Promote your event well in advance. Invite as broad a swath of the school and your community as possible (colleagues, families, classmates, local officials).

- Provide opportunities for a dress rehearsal before students present in a large public forum. This will build student confidence and give them a final opportunity to adjust their projects and presentations.

- Use your school's existing space. Reserve it well in advance. If it is too difficult to find a space to bring people together, consider using a virtual format to share student work. This time-saving approach can be more efficient and equally impactful as an in-person event.

- On the day of the expo, seek help in setting up. Invite your partners, colleagues, and students to join you.

- Provide food. Consider culturally relevant fare. It can calm student nerves and create community. Don't forget dessert for an end-of-event celebration.

- Ask students to come and set up their projects well before invited guests arrive.

- Consider using judges if a competitive atmosphere is desired. Use their evaluations to uplift exemplary work and celebrate all students who participated.

- Invite a keynote speaker from the project's focus area to talk with your students and the assembled audience. Doing so can connect the work students complete to that of real-world professionals.

- Look to infuse the expo with youth-led elements. Tap students to be Expo MCs (or create other roles—greeter, usher, judge correspondent, event photographer).

- Take pictures and videos (or have a student do it). The day after an event, relive the expo experience with your classroom. Show these images to the following year's expo participants so they know what to expect.

- Consider having students write thank-you notes to those who attended. Ask them to invite the audience back to next year's expo.

- Use a cross-classroom interdisciplinary approach to help create a more rigorous and robust expo. Invite colleagues from other content areas to use the expo format as an opportunity to co-create overlapping curricula and assessments. Science, English, civics, and history can work exceptionally well together, but other content combinations are equally if not more powerful.

- Turn your expo into a film festival (chapter 11). Teach students how to make documentaries. This can allow you to enact a critical media pedagogy approach that empowers students as storytellers. Essential components of filmmaking include proper planning and equipment, editing software, storyboarding, evidence-collection strategies and techniques, exemplars, and student critique.

Celebrations (Multiple Chapters, Chapter 12)

- Celebrations of learning are a way to acknowledge student work and share it publicly. They can take place in the classroom (with or without the presence of experts) or in a more public forum for the larger community. Regardless of how or where they occur, celebrations of learning should seek to signal to students that the work they are doing in the classroom matters to an audience wider than their classmates and teacher.

- Enter student work in contests. Doing so is not just another way to celebrate learning but also a way to make connections between the work taking place in the classroom and the real world. It can also lead to unexpected outcomes, including awards and opportunities to perform and present (chapter 4).

- Food can play a vital role in the learning process, particularly at the end of a unit or as part of a presentation or public gathering. Look for opportunities to use food to connect to a community's culture or push the boundaries of a student's palate. A satisfied stomach is a great way to make students feel comfortable, courageous, and celebrated.

- The work of a teacher is almost impossible and never-ending. Take time and make space to celebrate yourself, your students, and your colleagues. Celebrations of accomplishment are a great way to push back against feelings of demoralization, elevate and spread awareness of your message across a newly realized platform, recognize your colleagues, and inspire the next generation of educators.

Depending on where you are in your career as an educator, you might not consider every action or approach suitable for your classroom or curriculum. I acknowledge that possibility. However, regardless of how you view them, I hope that something from this guide resonates with you and helps you start, transform, or continue to improve the learning environment in your classroom for you and your students. Being an educator is not easy. It is nearly impossible, always messy, and best accomplished when you work with like-minded colleagues and collaborators. Indeed, that is why I wrote this book, and that is why I will be here (to the best of my ability) to support you on your educator journey.

Acknowledgments

Like teaching, writing a book is not possible without others. I have been fortunate and am tremendously grateful to have crossed paths with, worked with, and garnered the support of an incredible network of individuals and organizations that have provided the impetus and ideas for this book.

First and foremost, this book was only possible because of the Washington Heights Expeditionary Learning School community (a.k.a. the WHEELS Family). Teaching at WHEELS for over a decade, a school founded by and for teachers, was where I rubbed elbows with a host of like-minded colleagues and found my home as an educator.

While the collective support I gained by working in a community like WHEELS was paramount, there are two colleagues and dear friends, Anthony Voulgarides and Erick Espin, whom I leaned heavily upon both in the classroom and when writing this book. Collectively, Anthony and Erick are the greatest teachers I have ever had the experience of working with. They are masters of their craft, inspirational educators, and incredible human beings. Working with Anthony and Erick made me a better teacher and person. Their enthusiasm and excitement for collaboration, curriculum, and working with students were infectious in the best possible way. I hope all educators and students soon find their own Mr. V and Mr. Espin.

A recurrent theme throughout this book and a hallmark of my teaching practice was the reliance on and partnership with an incredible network of individuals and organizations. I loved inviting outside experts into my classroom. From a personal standpoint, I always learned something new, and from the perspective of my students, classroom visitors made what they were learning more enjoyable and exciting. Partnering with experts was the ultimate synergistic multiplier, magnifying my ability to teach in an impactful and positive way.

One of the best things about partnering with outside organizations was that my students and I had the pleasure of interacting with many exceptional individuals. To these individuals and the organizations they represented through their participation in my classroom, thank you for joining us in partnership and in pursuit of learning science and bettering the environment around us.

I must acknowledge the following individuals and organizations, by general order of their appearance in this book (note: some individuals are no longer employed by the organization they are listed with):

Bronx River Alliance.

Catskill Watershed Corporation and the Ashokan Center.

Sean Miller.

NYC H$_2$O—Matt Malina, Stalin Espinal, Kevin Barrett, Steve Duncan, David Chuchuca, Amelia Zaino, and others.

The entire education programming department at the New York City Department of Environmental Protection and Beau Ranheim and Jih Shyu of the Marine Sciences Division.

WE ACT for Environmental Justice—Peggy Shepard, Evelyn Joseph, Ogonnaya Dotson-Newman, David Chang, Milagros de Hoz, and more. A special shout-out to Beau Morton—the ultimate curriculum collaborator, workshop facilitator, co-teacher, and visionary who helped sustain our EJ Expo over multiple years.

BioBus.

The Billion Oyster Project.

Futures Ignite—thank you, molly delano, for your visionary leadership and for seeing opportunities others would have overlooked. To Génesis Abreu, your environmental justice efforts and our continued partnership are a source of soul-nourishing inspiration.

New York Restoration Project—to Jason Smith, thank you for taking that initial leap of faith in deciding to work with my classroom all those years ago and collaborate with us to beautify and renew Highbridge Park and 182nd Street.

Educational Video Center.

Thank you to the organizations that support and uplift the teaching profession. I value your work more than you know and encourage others to follow in your trailblazing footsteps—Math for America, the Alfred P. Sloan Foundation, the Fund for the City of New York, the Academy for Teachers, the Summer Research Program for Science Teachers at Columbia University, and the American Museum for Natural History.

As a first-time book author, I am grateful for the support of the professionals, colleagues, and industry experts who have guided me through the book writing process and publishing journey.

Michael Signorelli at Aevitas Creative Management. It has been a pleasure and quite the experience to bring our past teamwork on the soccer field into the literary world.

At Beacon Press, executive editor Rachael Marks and editorial assistant Rebecca Johnson—thank you for believing in the stories and lessons in this book. Thank you for your critical eye and editorial suggestions. Your support and guidance pushed me and this book to a higher level. Thank you as well to the production team that helped move my writing from manuscript to book. Much appreciation to production manager Beth Collins, managing editor Susan Lumenello, and copyeditor Brian Baughan. Thank you as well to sales and marketing coordinators Frankie Karnedy and Brittany Wallace. Thank you to my Beacon publicist, Perpetua Cannistraro. And thank you to Louis Roe for the incredible book cover art and design. Your combined professionalism and expertise represent everything a publishing house should be.

Nevin Martell—your sound and sage advice were wise and always helpful.

The idea of writing a book does not happen without an initial injection of suggestion and ongoing doses of encouragement and persuasion.

For the initial spark that ignited the concept of this book, I must thank the brilliant Chris Emdin. When I was still a doctoral student under his tutelage, struggling to navigate the dissertation process, Chris envisioned this book's reality. Thank you, Chris, for planting this seed of encouragement. Thank you for suggesting and vouching for me to Beacon Press. Thank you for writing the foreword to this book.

For ongoing doses of motivation, I must thank Nick Piombino. My oracle of optimism, sounding board, and therapeutic construer of confidence.

To my immediate family, I love you.

To my mother—your countless hours spent at home preparing your lessons on the living room floor, and the opportunity I had to be a part of your classroom as your substitute teacher served as a model for what it looks like to dedicate oneself to their students and a career in education.

Poppy, Ollie, and Benji—you are the greatest teachers I have ever had. Your dad loves you to the moon and back again.

To Yom—my partner in life, learning, and love. You are brilliant, compassionate, and a force of nature in every way. As an educator, your passion transforms learning environments; as a mother, your love shapes our family; and as my partner, you inspire me daily. The Wee Foxes and I are beyond lucky to share life's adventures with you. Thank you, for you. Love, always.

Notes

Introduction

1. Francesca Costa, "An 'Oft-Repeated Anecdote': A 'Cliff Notes' Story," Palisades Interstate Park Commission, March 2022, https://www.njpalisades.org/oft RepeatedAnecdote.html.

2. Environment and Health Data Portal, "Outdoor Air and Health in Washington Heights," City of New York, https://a816-dohbesp.nyc.gov/IndicatorPu blic/neighborhood-reports/washington_heights/outdoor_air_and_health/, accessed February 23, 2024; Environment and Health Data Portal, "Asthma and the Environment in Washington Heights," NYC.gov, https://a816-dohbesp.nyc .gov/IndicatorPublic/neighborhood-reports/washington_heights/asthma_and _the_environment/, accessed February 23, 2024.

Chapter 1: Field Trips, Localized Learning, and Students as Scientists

1. David J. Lizotte et al., "Usable Assessments Aligned with Curriculum Materials: Measuring Explanation as a Scientific Way of Knowing," paper presented at the annual meeting of the American Educational Research Association (AERA), Chicago, IL, April 2003, http://websites.umich.edu/~hiceweb/PDFs/2003/Lizot te_rubrics_AERA2003.pdf.

2. "Bronx," Poetry.com, https://www.poetry.com/poem/56007/bronx, accessed February 26, 2024.

Chapter 2: The Hook and the Circle

1. US Department of Health and Human Services, "Surgeon General Issues New Advisory About Effects Social Media Use Has on Youth Mental Health," press release, May 5, 2023, https://www.hhs.gov/about/news/2023/05/23/surge on-general-issues-new-advisory-about-effects-social-media-use-has-youth-me ntal-health.html; Jonathan Haidt, *The Anxious Generation: How the Great Rewiring of Childhood Is Causing an Epidemic of Mental Illness* (New York: Penguin Press, 2024).

2. Project Zero's Thinking Routine Toolbox, Harvard Graduate School of Education, https://pz.harvard.edu/thinking-routines, accessed November 5, 2024.

3. "What's Your Water Footprint?" Water Footprint Calculator, https://www.watercalculator.org/, accessed November 5, 2024.

4. Tina Rosenberg, "The Burden of Thirst," *National Geographic*, April 1, 2010, 102–11.

5. Matt Copeland, *Socratic Circles: Fostering Critical and Creative Thinking in Middle and High School* (New York: Routledge, 2005).

Chapter 3: An Exploration of New York City's Water Supply

1. NYC Environmental Protection, "History of New York City Drinking Water," City of New York, https://www.nyc.gov/site/dep/water/history-of-new-york-citys-drinking-water.page/, accessed November 5, 2024.

2. Matthew P. White et al., "Spending at Least 120 Minutes a Week in Nature Is Associated with Good Health and Wellbeing," *Scientific Reports* 9, no. 7730 (June 2019), https://doi.org/10.1038/s41598-019-44097-3.

3. NYC Environmental Protection, *New York City Drinking Water Supply and Quality Report 2022*, City of New York, https://www.nyc.gov/assets/dep/down loads/pdf/water/drinking-water/drinking-water-supply-quality-report/2022 -drinking-water-supply-quality-report.pdf.

Chapter 4: Experts in the Classroom

1. Simon Scarr and Marco Hernandez, "Drowning in Plastic: Visualizing the World's Addition to Plastic," Reuters Graphics, September 4, 2019, https://www.reuters.com/graphics/ENVIRONMENT-PLASTIC/0100B275155/index.html.

2. *The Story of Bottled Water*, Louis Fox, dir., Free Range Studios, March 2010, 8 min., https://www.storyofstuff.org/movies/story-of-bottled-water/.

3. International Bottled Water Association, "Bottled Water Reaches New Peaks in Revenue and Volume," press release, https://bottledwater.org/nr/bottled-water-reaches-new-peaks-in-revenue-and-volume/, accessed November 5, 2024.

4. *Tapped*, Stephanie Soechtig and Jason Lindsey, dirs., Atlas Films, May 2009, 76 min.

Chapter 5: Exploring City Sewers

1. Peter A. Cohen, James A. Kulik, and Chen-Lin C. Kulik, "Educational Outcomes of Tutoring: A Meta-analysis of Findings," *American Education Research Journal* 19, no 2 (January 1982): 165–81, https://doi.org/10.3102/00028312019 002237.

Chapter 6: The Critical Examination of a Harbor's Health

1. "What Is the Winkler Method for Dissolved Oxygen?" Atlas Scientific Environmental Robotics, September 28, 2022, https://atlas-scientific.com/blog/winkler-method-for-dissolved-oxygen/.

2. NYC Environmental Protection, *New York Harbor Water Quality Report*, City of New York, 2018, https://www.nyc.gov/assets/dep/downloads/pdf/water/nyc-waterways/harbor-water-quality-report/2018-new-york-harbor-water-quality-report.pdf.

3. Jack Lewis, "The Spirit of the First Earth Day," *EPA Journal* 16 (1990): 8; US Environmental Protection Agency, "The Origins of EPA," last updated May 31, 2024, https://www.epa.gov/history/origins-epa; US Environmental Protection Agency, "Clean Air Act Requirements and History," last updated August 6, 2024, https://www.epa.gov/clean-air-act-overview/clean-air-act-requirements-and-history; US Environmental Protection Agency, "History of the Clean Water Act," last updated June 12, 2024, https://www.epa.gov/laws-regulations/history-clean-water-act.

4. New York City Department of Environmental Protection, "DEP Marks 100th Anniversary of the Harbor Survey Program: Centennial Report Shows New York Harbor Is the Cleanest in a Century," press release, November 10, 2010. https://www.nyc.gov/html/dep/html/press_releases/10-96pr.shtml.

5. "Combined Sewage Overflows (CSOs)," Riverkeeper, https://www.riverkeeper.org/campaigns/stop-polluters/sewage-contamination/cso/, accessed November 5, 2024.

6. NYC Environmental Protection, "Wastewater Treatment System," City of New York, https://www.nyc.gov/site/dep/water/wastewater-treatment-system.page/, accessed November 5, 2024.

Chapter 7: In Pursuit of Environmental Justice

1. Angelica I. Tiotiu et al., "Impact of Air Pollution on Asthma Outcomes," *International Journal of Environmental Research and Public Health* 19, no. 2 (January 1982): 237–48, https://doi.org/10.3102/00028312019002237.

Chapter 8: Shifting Baselines and Gazes

1. Mark D. Binder, Nobutaka Hirokawa, and Uwe Windhorst, eds., "Gaze Shift," in *Encyclopedia of Neuroscience* (Berlin: Springer, 2009), https://doi.org/10.1007/978-3-540-29678-2_1941.

2. City of New York Parks & Recreation, *Natural Area Mapping and Inventory of Highbridge Park: Final Report*, https://www.nycgovparks.org/sub_about/

parks_divisions/nrg/documents/Ecological%20Assessment%20-%20Highbridge%20Park.pdf, accessed November 5, 2024.

3. "History of the American Chestnut Tree," American Chestnut Foundation, https://tacf.org/history-american-chestnut/, accessed November 5, 2024.

4. Iovanni Romarion, "I'm a Student Climate Activist in NYC. The Fight Is Local, and It's Personal," *Chalkbeat*, August 5, 2022, https://www.chalkbeat.org/newyork/2022/8/5/23287853/nyc-storm-climate-change-activism-washington-heights/.

Chapter 9: The Classroom Is Your Oyster

1. Homi K. Bhabha, *The Location of Culture* (London: Routledge, 1994); Edward Soja, *Thirdspace: Journeys to Los Angeles and Other Real-and-Imagined Places* (Oxford: Basil Blackwell, 1996).

2. Jared Fox, "Changes in Urban Youths' Attitude Towards Science and Perception of a Mobile Science Lab Experience," PhD diss., Columbia University, 2015, https://doi.org/10.7916/D85Q4V5X.

Chapter 10: Maps and Apps

1. US Government Accountability Office, *K–12 Education: Student Population Has Significantly Diversified, But Many Schools Remain Divided Along Racial, Ethnic, and Economic Lines*, Report to the Chairman, Committee on Education and Labor, US House of Representatives, published June 16, 2022, https://www.gao.gov/products/gao-22-104737.

2. US Government Accountability Office, *K–12 Education: Public High Schools with More Students in Poverty and Smaller Schools Provide Fewer Academic Offerings to Prepare for College*, Report to the Ranking Member, Committee on Education and the Workforce, US House of Representatives, published October 11, 2018, https://www.gao.gov/products/gao-19-8.

Chapter 11: From Isolated Islands to a Connected Archipelago

1. Some of these films can be seen online. See WHEELS Senior Expedition YouTube page, https://www.youtube.com/@wheelsseniorexpedition1504.

2. Ernest Morrell, Rudy Duenas, Veronica Garcia, and Jorge Lopez, *Critical Media Pedagogy: Teaching for Achievement in City Schools* (New York: Teachers College Press, 2013).

Chapter 12: Celebrate Your Success

1. Doris Santoro, *Demoralized: Why Teachers Leave the Profession They Love and How They Can Stay* (Cambridge, MA: Harvard Education Press, 2018), 179–80.

2. Santoro, *Demoralized*, 179–80.

3. Santoro, *Demoralized*, 117.

4. Fund for the City of New York, "FCNY: Sloan STEM Awards 2019: JARED FOX," YouTube, March 23, 2021, https://www.youtube.com/watch?v=3liGlRZa jCk&t=5s.

5. Diane Arevalo, Ricardo Herrera, and Mayerling Lantigua, "Hope for the Decade: Our Vision for Climate Justice," *Manhattan Times*, January 13, 2020, https://www.manhattantimesnews.com/hope-for-the-decadeesperanza-para-la -decada/.

After the Classroom

1. Sandra Cisneros, *A House of My Own: Stories from My Life* (New York: Vintage Books, 2015), 277.

Actions and Approaches for Connecting Classrooms to the Real World

1. Rachel N. Arbor and Kevin Matteson, "Interdisciplinary Nature Journaling Improves Mood and Helps Build Connection in Middle School Students," *Environmental Education Research* (2024): 1–11, doi:10.1080/13504622.2024.24 05901.

2. Introducing New Topics with the Building Background Knowledge Workshop, EL Education, https://eleducation.org/resources/introducing-new-topics -with-the-building-background-knowledge-workshop.

Index